SHELTON STATE COMMUNITY
  COLLEGE
JUNIOR COLLEGE DIVISION
  LIBRARY

DISCARDED

HT   Bartholomew, Harland, 1889-
123
.B3   Land uses in American cities

DATE DUE			

LAND USES IN AMERICAN CITIES

HARVARD CITY PLANNING STUDIES, XV

University City, Missouri, showing areas developed in conformity with
the zoning plan. Courtesy of Papin Aerial Service, St. Louis

LAND USES

DISCARDED

IN AMERICAN CITIES

Harland Bartholomew

ASSISTED BY JACK WOOD

HARVARD UNIVERSITY PRESS ● CAMBRIDGE

© Copyright, 1955, by the President and Fellows of Harvard College

Third Printing, 1971

Distributed in Great Britain by
Oxford University Press, London

Library of Congress Catalog Card Number 55-5059
SBN 674-50900-5
Printed in the United States of America

The power to direct their growth and advancement came to American cities at a late stage in their development. Between 1916 and 1929, many cities adopted zoning plans in an endeavor to curb the excesses resulting from rapid, uncontrolled growth, and to bring about a more orderly pattern of development. Since this administrative device was both new in the field of municipal law and untested in the courts, it was gingerly applied. It was not until the decision of the United States Supreme Court in the now famous Euclid Village case of 1926, that zoning was clearly established as a proper exercise of the police power.

Most of the early zoning plans bear the imprint of the handicaps under which they were drafted. There was an uncertainty as to the character and extent of the regulations that would be upheld in the courts of law. They were drafted during a period when cities were growing rapidly and speculative pressures were at their greatest. Moreover, there was a striking lack of knowledge of the amount of land required for urban development.

In 1932, in an endeavor to meet the need for factual data on the use of urban land, Harvard University and its School of City Planning sponsored publication of statistical material compiled from zoning surveys in sixteen central cities and six satellite cities. This material forms Volume IV of its City Planning Studies, titled *Urban Land Uses.*

Twenty years have passed since this early research was undertaken. In this period, American cities have experienced a severe economic depression, a sustained period of retarded growth, a resurgence of growth stemming from the tremendous industrial expansion necessitated by World War II and, more recently, an unprecedented areal expansion caused by the widespread use of the passenger auto-

mobile. Each of these developments created problems not anticipated in former zoning regulations. Meanwhile, with wider experience, zoning techniques were expanded and improved.

Cities have found it desirable as well as necessary to revise their
zoning plans. So long as the city is dynamic, zoning must be studied
and adjusted periodically if it is to function properly. Since 1932,
detailed data of land use in some fifty-three central cities and thirty-
three satellite communities have been compiled by my office. It is
hoped that this larger volume of information, covering a much
wider range of cities than was possible in the 1932 edition, will
prove helpful in the continuing study of the American city and as
an aid to improved zoning practice. It is possible now to compare
land use characteristics in cities of varying sizes. The data here
presented for central cities are divided into four groups: cities of less
than 50,000; of 50,000 to 100,000; of 100,000 to 250,000; and of
more than 250,000 in population. In addition, information has
been gathered for several complete urban areas. Data for eleven
central cities *and* their total fringe development—that is, for eleven
complete metropolitan areas—have been compiled and are shown
herein.

The services of many persons over a long period of time have
been required to prepare and analyze the voluminous statistics contained in this volume. Many staff members have been employed in
the field surveys, and in recording and processing the survey data.
Special acknowledgment is made of the services of Earle H. Franke
for numerous field surveys and for extensive tabulation throughout
the entire twenty-year period covered by this study. James Appel
undertook analysis of statistical material and some earlier textual
matter. Much helpful assistance in all phases of the work has been
given by my esteemed associates, Russell H. Riley, Harry W. Alex-
ander, and Eldridge H. Lovelace. For assistance in the preparation
of final text and tables, I wish to make grateful acknowledgment
of the services of Jack Wood, a valued member of my staff. Helpful
suggestions and valuable comments on the text have also been made
by William L. C. Wheaton and are also gratefully acknowledged.

H. B.

St. Louis, 1953

CONTENTS

TABLES

LAND USES IN AMERICAN CITIES

1

INTRODUCTION

The growth of large centers of population and the speed at which they have spread, overflowing their boundaries, and forming sprawling agglomerations of buildings and people are products of modern times. In the United States the rapidity of urbanization has accentuated our urban problems. Despite the enormous significance of urban life in our society, our knowledge of the city and of the process of urbanization is conspicuously incomplete. The momentum behind urban growth—the social and industrial forces that draw people to the city—is difficult to direct or to control. To do so requires the most positive planning and administrative measures.

THE PLANNING CONCEPT

The city is a relatively large, dense, and permanent settlement of individuals engaged in diverse economic activities. With the great growth of the large urban unit in the last century, the term "city" has attained a broader meaning; for while the city is the traditional center of urbanism, the urban way of life exists as much today in the smaller town as in the large metropolitan areas. The history of urbanization in the United States is largely one of economic change and social adjustment, and of the attempts of the individual to fit his activities to these changing conditions. In this process many maladjustments occur. The problems that arise are those which urban planning seeks to remedy.

Clearly, in the study of the city we are dealing with a complex of human activities. The scope of these activities, as well as their complexity, distorts our concept of urban organization. Seldom is the city thought of as something more than an administrative unit, or the urban aggregation as more than a geographic or political enigma. Thus, while attempts to mitigate the evils of congestion and disorganization produced a multitude of "city-betterment" movements, these attempts often lacked a basic understanding of urban problems. It is not surprising, then, that the early attacks on community disorganization, however worthy, were uncoördinated and, thus, seldom fully effective.

Yet it was through these piecemeal attempts to deal with the many facets of the problem that the interrelationship of each element in the urban scene—housing to sanitation, open space to health, the city structure to economics, etc.—was recognized, and the value of planning acknowledged. Generally, there is in each community some form of planning and organization of activities based on tradition and custom. But while conventions have served as guides to community development in earlier times, these have proved inadequate to contain and to give proper direction to the overwhelming city growth experienced in the past century. The growth of population, advances in technology, and the rapidity of change itself caused this empirical planning to be supplanted by more deliberate guidance of urban development.

This does not suggest that planning, either city or regional, has reached its maturity. Clearly it has not. Nor has it kept pace with our social, economic, and technical advance. Even so, urban planning as it is practiced today has moved far from its humble beginnings. Today, most community development is guided or influenced by planning in some degree. Yet there is little occasion for complacency. Sound urban planning involves the coördination of manifold activities and the orderly arrangement of space for their proper functioning. It involves the adjustment of these activities for better service to the community as a whole, as well as for the highest possible satisfaction of the needs of the private individual in our free society.

Thus urban planning as now envisioned is more than a palliative applied to past errors in city building. It has become a device by which an attempt is made to provide for present and future social and economic needs in a more orderly fashion. Here is the justification for planning; in it is the virility of the planning movement.

THE GROWTH AND NATURE OF THE PLANNING PROCESS

The growth of modern planning has been a slow and often tortuous attempt to eliminate the incongruities of the Industrial Revolution—and its corollary, urban congestion. It began, as many reforms do, in a negative spirit. Increasingly intolerable living conditions stimulated reforms in housing and sanitation. The public health acts that resulted were our first attempts to define minimum standards for urban areas. These included sanitation requirements, building regulations, housing controls, etc.—standards now inherent in the sphere of planning. There was, however, a serious weakness. Although these reforms were developed simultaneously, it was little realized how they were interrelated, for each was viewed as a separate problem. Subsequently, the provision of parks, improved transportation facilities, and civic architecture became parallel movements, marking a period in our planning history characterized by its preoccupation with anesthetics and often described by the term "city beautiful."

The need for a comprehensive treatment of the urban problem as a means to a better living environment was highlighted at the first national conference on city planning in 1909. Emphasizing the economic rather than the aesthetic point of view, this conference marked a turning point in planning. In the decades to follow planning became "practical" as well as visually appealing, and applicable to private land and facilities as well as to public undertakings. But sweeping as these changes were, planning was still largely confined to the physical design of land and its appurtenances.

Within recent years planning has taken on a much broader significance. Brought into sharp focus by the economic depression of the 1930's, the social and economic maladjustments of our urban areas attracted nationwide attention and, incidentally, the intervention of the federal government in the field of local planning. The depression was undoubtedly instrumental in reorientating and stimulating improved planning for our cities. Over the past twenty years commendable, but only partially successful, efforts have been made to deal with the total urban problem. Today the location of industry, the erosion of social values in slums, and the economic drain on our large cities from sprawling fringe developments are just as vital concerns of planning as the location of a trunk sewer or a civic building.

In sum, planning has advanced far since the day when it meant little more than civic embellishment. Today, planning is a powerful tool for shaping the urban structure, and its use is recognized as a significant function of local government. It is a device for coördinating many of the activities of local government, and finally, it is a positive guide to community redevelopment and growth.

ZONING

Like most problems of social control, planning could not be fully implemented without public sanction in the form of legislation. This authorization in the United States is contained in the police power of the community. It is through the use of this power to promote the general welfare of the community as well as the public health and safety that we regulate building materials and methods by building ordinances, and control land use through zoning, subdivision control, and other planning measures. Zoning is perhaps the most important of these, both as a social control device and in its wide effects on land use.

The proper function of zoning is first, to control the use of land and buildings and, second, to regulate the size and shape of buildings and their relation to each other. Zoning, as the word suggests, describes the areas within which these controls are enforced. Use regulations allocate to each major type of activity land which is sufficient and appropriate for that purpose; districts given to heavy industrial use are segregated from commercial areas; residential districts are protected from the invasion of commerce and industry; and the district established for one type of residential use is separated from other types and densities of residential uses.

Land coverage, population density, and height of buildings are prescribed for each zone type. The limits imposed prevent congestion and maintain needed light, air, and open space. It is equally important that these limits on density of development should tend to mitigate the congestion of vehicular traffic. By these controls zoning regulations protect the desirable character of development in each district, stabilize real estate values and the community tax base, and assure the most economic provision of municipal services and utilities.

The development of zoning has been rapid in recent years. The courts, cognizant of the role of urban planning, have contributed to the advancement of zoning through their broadened interpretation of the police power. Whereas the early conception of the function of zoning was in a sense as an extension of the principle of nuisance control—and somewhat later as a means of protecting residential property—the modern view sees zoning functions as a tool for comprehensive planning. Thus visualized, it is now possible to prescribe the use of land within definite limits.

We can now determine land requirements with an assurance that these will be balanced with other community needs. Zoning, since it can now be employed in a truly positive and constructive sense, has become an effective guide to social development.

The rapid acceptance of zoning as a device for guiding urban growth is indicated by the fact that not until 1916 was an American city comprehensively zoned; whereas, at present, most communities have some form of zoning. Originating in Europe, zoning was first used in the United States about the turn of the century when Washington, Boston, and Los Angeles used fragmentary codes to limit height of buildings and restrict the location of certain uses. Comprehensive zoning began in 1916 with the passage of the New York City ordinance. Since then, the principle of zoning has become firmly entrenched in the American community and, more recently, has been extended to rural areas. Several states have enacted legislation permitting county and township zoning, which in effect permits, for the first time, the application of zoning control to all land, both rural and urban.

The usefulness of zoning, however, has not been fully explored. Despite the widespread use of comprehensive zoning, the problems with which the zoning ordinance must cope are constantly changing. The development of airports has required new protective regulations. Building is no longer confined to an individual lot, but often becomes an operation covering an entire block or an area of several blocks. Automobile traffic has swamped inadequate street systems. The character of industrial and commercial operations has changed with the emergence of the landscaped plant site and the suburban shopping center. As a result of these changes, revised zoning ordinances frequently contain many new specifications providing for airport approach areas, off-street parking, vehicle loading spaces, transitional use zones, and the elimination of nonconforming uses.

These devices have not been fully successful; nor have they covered all of the new problems constantly emerging. These problems challenge the resourcefulness of planning and highlight the need for improved zoning methods.

The full use of zoning is not yet apparent. There has been a reluctance in most communities to press for a full use of such controls. Paradoxically, the latitude generally permitted by the courts has been broad enough to permit important innovations of planning. Indeed, it is the opinion of some students that it is the conservatism of planners in drafting zoning codes and of legislative bodies in their enactments, rather than the necessary caution of the courts, that have prescribed the limits of zoning. The perpetuation of nonconforming uses and the use of the Board of Adjustment to circumvent the regulations are cases in point. There is an obvious need for rethinking the matter. In this process further legal clarification by the courts may be a means to more effective zoning—and to better communities.

Zoning has met with a substantial degree of success, however, and is a legally established if not altogether politically accepted practice. The history of zoning is replete with legal findings growing out of individual or public controversy. However, only those questions bearing on the relations between urban land use and zoning need concern us here.

In devising and applying zoning schemes to the urban complex we are confronted with several practical problems, the greatest of which is the task of comprehending and enveloping in the zoning scheme the diverse forces of urbanization. The determination of land use requirements and spatial distribution of the uses is a prerequisite to zoning, Indeed, this is perhaps the most difficult of all city planning endeavors, for urban areas are extremely complex units which cannot be easily analyzed into all their components, nor wholly explained by logical reasoning. Some have grown more slowly, some more rapidly, but all under varying pressures. Through a process of growth and decay, trial and error, cities have met reasonably well a wide variety of demands. Our cities function surprisingly well despite the fact that the land use pattern is the end result of the activities of innumerable individuals, each acting independently and largely without consciousness of any overall pattern.

In planning and zoning we are attempting to achieve a consistent and orderly pattern of growth. Planning is the task of producing by foresight and skill what has previously been left to the interplay of individual actions. Rather than endure the painfully slow and wasteful process of a natural succession of uses, we are attempting to predetermine a logical land use pattern. Of course, zoning should reflect so far as possible the city dweller's idea of the kind of community he wishes to live in; however, this is not the total problem. The individual and collective desires of the community can find expression in the zoning scheme. But the urban area is a product of forces over which we seem to have only limited conscious control. The demand for urban land is inextricably related to the growth characteristics and spatial distribution of the population, to social behavior and habits, and to economic functions. A zoning plan should reflect these forces and the demands they make on the services of land, as well as the highly personal needs of each citizen. Depreciated land values and blight can and have resulted from zoning plans based on unsound assumptions concerning the direction and extent of civic growth.

The urban complex is, figuratively, an organism that cannot maintain its equilibrium if forced too far from its natural pattern. Thus, zoning can do little to modify the basic forces that produce the demands for land. Rather, it must be a rationalization and expression of these forces—beginning with a clear understanding of the pattern of land uses.

TYPES OF CITIES

Within the past few decades we have seen a dramatic change in the form of urban settlement. Beginning with improved methods of transportation—notably the automobile—the city has changed from a compact unit to a more open and less intensively developed area. The city has, in effect, spread over a larger and larger area until the original settlement has lost its identity, becoming in this new form the nucleus of a much larger center of population.

Three components of the urban area can be identified: the central city, the satellite or suburban city, and the politically undefined fringe development lying between the city and the country. In character, each of these areas is distinct but not separate, for each is a part of the modern urban community. Each of these parts is of interest here. So that we may see something of the change that has taken place as cities have expanded, this study will follow the sequence of the growth pattern of the urban area. First, we will consider the central city, then the suburban city or satellite, and lastly, the entire urban area.

The term "central city" here refers to the municipality in which is centered the major social and economic activities of an urban area. It is largely a self-sufficient city, but one that may have in recent years attracted a sprawl of fringe development not yet absorbed in the corporate limits of the city.

The "satellite city" is a community adjacent to a larger municipality. While the satellite city has a separate political existence, it is in one degree or another dependent on the central city for its economic and cultural well-being. It may take the form of a "dormitory" suburb with many of its inhabitants employed in the central city, or it may be largely an industrial suburb drawing workers from other areas.

The "urban area," on the other hand, is not a political or governmental unit, but includes the central city, any satellite community, and all developed area within the urban fringe.

SCOPE OF THIS RESEARCH

The statistical and graphic information in the following chapters was derived from uniform land use field surveys conducted during the past two decades. These surveys covered eighty-six cities and eleven urban areas. Of the former, fifty-three are central cities and thirty-three, satellite cities. In population, the central cities range from 1,740 in Naples, Fla., to 821,960 in St. Louis, Mo. The city of Northfield, Ill., with a population of only 900, is the smallest of the satellite communities studied, whereas East St. Louis, Ill., with

PLATE I. Geographic location of cities and urban areas

LEGEND

• CENTRAL CITIES
○ SATELLITE CITIES
▲ URBAN AREAS

74,347 is the largest. The urban area centering on Corpus Christi, Tex., is the largest of eleven areas surveyed. It has a population of 119,825 persons.*

To show the characteristics of cities differing in size, all cities have been grouped by size as well as by type, as follows.

AREA SURVEYED	POPULATION GROUP	NUMBER OF AREAS
Central cities	50,000 or less	27
	50,000 – 100,000	13
	100,000 – 250,000	8
	250,000 and over	5
Satellite cities	5,000 or less	7
	5,000 – 10,000	6
	10,000 – 25,000	10
	25,000 and over	10
Urban areas	120,000 or less	11

Data concerning each of the individual cities and urban areas surveyed are contained in Appendix A.

Geographically, most sections of the country are represented in the research, although cities of the Middle West predominate. The geographic distribution of the cities covered is illustrated on Plate I. No attempt has been made to group the cities and the data for each community by regions. Nor is it implied that this is an exhaustive survey that will produce an answer to fit any or all cities, for it will not. However, the cities surveyed do represent a wide cross section of American cities—diverse in size, character, and location †—from which we can make observations of existing use of land and get some idea of the trends in land utilization. These data are of value not only in urban planning, but also in annexation studies, real estate surveys of various kinds, market determinations, and many other types of inquiry.

* The population figures are taken from the most recent U. S. census at the time the city was surveyed, or estimated for the year of survey.

† Perhaps the city with the least characteristic land use pattern is Williamsburg, Virginia. Since this community is a historical shrine and possesses an unusually high amount of public and semipublic development typical of such centers, many of the percentages and ratios for this city found in the analyses of the various land uses deviate widely from the norm. However, since Williamsburg is a small community the statistical data concerning it does not greatly affect any of the group averages.

2

THE LAND USE SURVEY

Cities have grown largely as a result of industrial activities that require a concentrated population. It follows that urban land is required for these activities and for housing. Knowledge of the composition of the urban area is a prerequisite to rational planning and zoning. This planning requires both knowledge of the broad characteristics of the urban pattern and quantitative analysis of the space devoted to each type of land use.

THE EVOLUTION OF LAND USES

Urban communities have developed as a part of our social and economic system. The amount of land utilized by specific activities and their spatial distribution reflect the requirements of this system. In our communities, however, the existing arrangement of land uses, though essentially functional, is not a criterion of modern community design. The pattern is, to a large extent, a product of past growth and activities; it does not necessarily represent the most efficient pattern. This is understandable, for urban areas have grown under varying pressures and have been subjected to a multitude of personal whims and desires. Yet, despite the lack of formal planning in early cities, the land use pattern that has evolved is essentially functional.

The community is a dynamic organism constantly changing in a variety of ways to meet new needs and conditions. The change that has occurred in one community is illustrated in Plate II. As

11

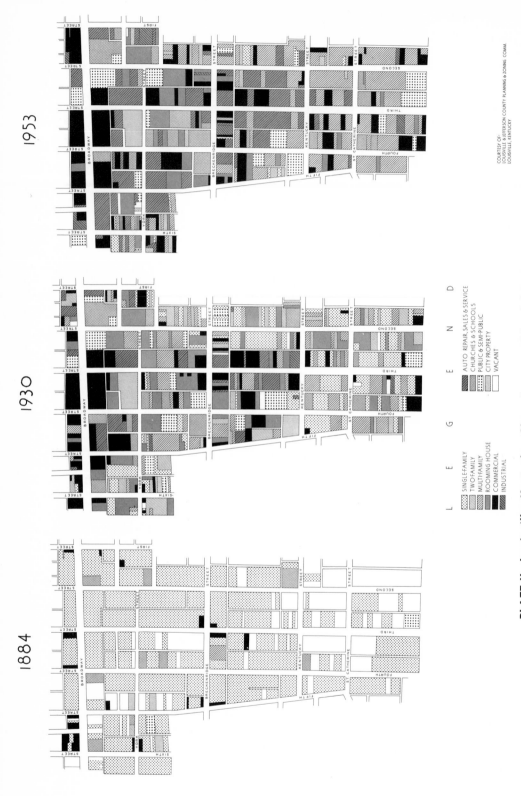

PLATE II. Louisville, Kentucky. Changing use of land during a seventy-year
period. Courtesy of Louisville and Jefferson County Planning and Zoning.

the community grows older its physical parts become obsolete and should be rebuilt. With each technical improvement they become less efficient and a change in the utilization of land inevitably occurs. Moreover, as the community ages, there are progressive changes in the social and economic structure, in the characteristics of the population, in the size of families, in age composition, and in the nature of occupations. These tend to produce new and different demands on the service of land.

But the greatest change in the urban community is perhaps a result of growth itself. With the increase in population through natural accrual or by migration, new living and working space must be added to the community. This demand may be satisfied by peripheral expansion, by the internal rearrangement of land uses—either through the displacement of one use by another or by the infilling of vacant property—or by the more intensive use of land and existing buildings. These latter growth processes are relatively slow and are more characteristic of high value areas, such as central commercial or industrial districts commanding good market prices. More often, community growth flows into areas offering the least physical or economic resistance to expansion. Thus the predominant type of growth occurs in the form of lateral expansion into surrounding agricultural areas where raw land is converted to urban purposes.

Whatever the nature of the growth, it is apparent that the land use pattern, as well as the amount of land utilized for a particular purpose, and often the density of development, are constantly undergoing change. Part of this change may be superficial, but most is a direct response to the changing needs of the community.

TYPES OF LAND USE

In the study of urban land use, we are concerned with surface utilization; therefore we consider all land in the urban area to be either developed, or vacant, or water area. The term "developed" includes all land that is used for purposes that are recognized as urban in character, whether public or private in nature, and whether devoted to an open use such as parks or playgrounds, or to a site use such as residence, industry, or commerce. Vacant land is that not given over to any urban use even though it may be potentially available for development. Thus for our purposes, agricultural land is considered vacant land. Water areas include natural and artificial bodies of water and represent no urban use except when embraced within a park or recreational area. Broadly then, the land we are concerned with can be described as land now used for purposes that are characteristically urban.

All urban land may be classified according to its use. These uses, as illustrated graphically on Plate III, include residence, commerce, industry, streets, railroads, recreation centers, and public or semipublic facilities. All land may be placed for planning purposes in one or another of these groups. Land use classifications are defined in Appendix B.*

Broadly speaking, about one half of all land in urban use is privately developed; and the other half is in public use. In the preparation of the city plan the designer is concerned largely with the public land: streets, parks, schools, public buildings, and utilities (both public and private). In zoning it is important that the "load on the land" imposed by private development be in scale and in harmony with the usage of the public land and facilities. It is in this context that the several functional uses of land will be reviewed.

PRIVATELY DEVELOPED AREAS

These areas include land developed by private interests or by the public if operated in a private or proprietary capacity (for example, public housing, the use of which is essentially private in nature). Functional uses in this group include the following.

> Single-family dwellings
> Two-family dwellings
> Multifamily dwellings
> Commercial areas
> Light industry
> Heavy industry

The titles of these uses are largely self-explanatory; however, some exceptions should be noted. A single-family dwelling is a detached structure used for residence by one family or household

* The classifications in Appendix B are those used by the author's office.

14

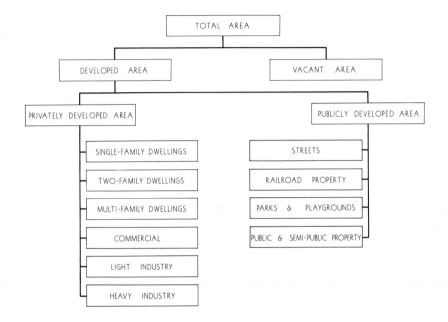

PLATE III. Uses of urban land

alone. Two-family dwellings include various forms of structures such as the "duplex" or the "semi-detached," but essentially any structure designed for or occupied by two households. Multifamily dwellings include tenements, apartments, and apartment hotels for nontransients, which house three or more families or households. Rooming and lodging houses are also included in this classification. It should be noted here that practical considerations in survey practices require a certain latitude. For example, it is not always possible to detect by inspection the incidental housing of one or two roomers in seemingly private dwellings. Thus single or two-family dwellings having two roomers or less are not altered in classification.

Commercial uses include all land and building wherein trade or business is conducted, for example, merchandising, business offices, amusement, and personal service uses.

Industry is divided into two types, light and heavy. Although these are not precisely appropriate terms, they are in common usage to distinguish unobjectionable industrial processes from those that are, or may become, objectionable in close proximity to other types of uses where people live or work. Thus, all industries that are known to emit smoke, dust, odor, or undue noise are classed as heavy industry. Conversely, other forms of manufacturing, storage, processing, or the like without these objectionable characteristics are classified as light industry.*

PUBLICLY DEVELOPED AREAS

Urban land in this group falls within the following broad classifications.

> Streets
> Railroad property
> Parks and playgrounds
> Public and semipublic property

Public and semipublic property includes city property, airports, public and private schools, churches and cemeteries, and other institutional property. This general category includes uses, developed either by public or private capital which may in fact be public

---

* The use of control devices such as smoke abatement units, air conditioning, etc., may permit the upgrading of some industries.

facilities or may be restricted, as in the case of private clubs, to a select group. However, in both cases a large number of people use the facility and the use is essentially public in nature.

The remaining portion of land within the urban area not included in the above groups of privately and publicly developed areas is unimproved vacant land and water areas. The meaning of these terms is evident; they are included in this study to give a comprehensive accounting of all acreage within the community, although as quantities they lack significance.

THE LAND USE SURVEY

A land use inventory and its analysis are essential tools in the preparation and administration of a comprehensive city plan. Knowledge of land use is more than a planning precept; it has legal significance. The community in exercising its planning and zoning powers must, as enabling acts put it, give "reasonable consideration to the character of each district and its particular suitability for particular uses."

As with all research, the land use survey should be planned and programmed in advance. The purpose of the survey should be identified and the amount of information and the degree of detail should be balanced against their ultimate use. Further, the survey technique should be standardized and the statistical and graphic form of data presentation determined.*

There are, of course, variations in the scope and techniques of land use surveys. The technique employed will depend on such factors as conditions peculiar to the community, the detail of information desired, and to some degree on personal preferences. However, the following method is in most common use, and is suitable for the majority of purposes.

The land use survey requires a field investigation. Prior to this field investigation, however, preliminary work should be done to obtain information as to street and lot lines, and such land use

---

* The land use survey is often employed as a means of collecting other basic data. For example, some cities have expanded the land use survey to include information on age and condition of structures and housing characteristics, which would be more properly termed "housing surveys" or "real property inventories." These are separate and distinct from the analysis of the *use* of land, with which this study is concerned.

data as may be secured from assessors' files, insurance atlases, real estate atlases, and aerial photographs. It is customary to record the desired information on a set of sectional maps usually having a scale of from one hundred to two hundred feet to the inch. In general, the field sheet must be of an adequate size to permit showing established property lines and dimensions as well as existing information and penciled notations.

The field investigation is a lot-by-lot inspection to determine specific land utilization. In older central city areas of mixed use greater care is required in determining uses than in newly developed sections of single-family detached dwellings. After the inspection of a parcel, its use is marked on the field sheet along with any necessary explanatory facts or comments. After completion of the field investigation the land use data on the field sheets is transferred to a final map. Usually this final "use map" is prepared in vivid colors to emphasize each of the separate types of use as well as the overall pattern. The field sheets are retained for reference and record purposes.

The final land use map depicts each classification or type of use of land in color or by an appropriate symbol representing a particular use classification. This map may be of sectional sheets, or it may be an overall map covering the entire area, or both. Since the draftsmanship of this map will be of high quality, the scale can be larger, up to, say, five hundred feet to the inch.

LAND USE ANALYSES

The applications of land use data for planning purposes are manifold. For example, they can be used to determine commercial markets, to locate institutions such as churches and schools, or for zoning purposes. Therefore, the type of statistical analysis in any given situation will be determined by the problems under study. In zoning studies, with which we are concerned here, it is essential to know the amount of land used for various purposes. Computations of lot and parcel areas, arranged according to each major type of use, should be made for individual blocks, then summarized for permanent unit areas or neighborhoods, and finally for the entire community. The result of these summaries is generally expressed as an area in acres, in percentages of total areas, and as a ratio of land used to given units of population. Zoning that is based on the facts of actual use of land will have far greater validity than that based upon opinions unsupported by such facts.

The land use map represents the conditions on a given date, and its validity becomes progressively less with each change in use of property. Thus, it is important to keep this graphic and statistical information current. In the interim, changes in land use can be recorded from building permits issued or from insurance atlas records; however, these are never fully effective. Periodic revisions, yearly if possible, should be made.

In conclusion, the value of land use surveys tabulated in the manner described lies in comparative statistics. But, as with all comparisons of this nature there are definite limits of applicability. A community's future land use requirements cannot be projected with complete accuracy on a basis of current ratios. Likewise, a comparison of land uses between two or more communities will disclose differences due to character and physiography. However, in both cases such comparisons can be instructive. In combination with other basic studies, and with good judgment, current land use data offers a factual base for improved planning and zoning practices.

3

THE CENTRAL CITY

Few American cities are contained within their official boundaries. The large metropolitan area is a mosaic of governmental units with haphazard lines of division but, on the whole, with a basic unity. The area found within each political subdivision of the metropolitan region is often an arbitrary or unnatural unit established with little regard for administrative organization or sound planning practices. The determination of the area to be included within each unit is controlled, on one hand, by the action of the city legislative body whose policy may be liberal or conservative or subject to frequent change, and, on the other hand, by state legislative enactments designed to restrict expansion.

The central city is defined by its official boundary and can be divided into its components of developed land, vacant land, and water areas. However, in the comparative study of land uses it is important to note that only in the amount of land developed for some urban use can significant comparisons be made. Water areas are varying physiographic features. Since corporate limits are arbitrary the amount of vacant land within the corporate limit is largely an arbitrary quantity and need not necessarily reflect the urban land market. Nevertheless, these areas are included in the study to give a complete accounting of the total city.

Data from the fifty-three land use surveys of central cities are tabulated in Tables 1 and 2. In addition, summaries by population group have been prepared and are shown in Tables 3 and 4. The data tabulated in Tables 1 and 3 show the area devoted to the major uses of urban land expressed as a percentage of the total developed area of the city, and then as a percentage of the total official city area. The data in Tables 2 and 4 also shows the area devoted to the major uses. The amount of land so used is expressed in these tables as a ratio of area to population, or specifically, acres per 100 persons.

DEVELOPED AREAS

Of the total area found within the boundaries of the fifty-three central cities only 55.85 per cent is developed for some urban use.* This relatively low utilization is visually apparent from Plate IV, on which the land use patterns for five central cities with populations ranging from 6,270 to 821,960 are illustrated. These cities, Woodward, Okla., Jacksonville, Ill., Lincoln, Neb., Utica, N. Y, and St. Louis, Mo., have been selected as cities typical of their size groups.

It is readily established from the accompanying tables that there
* The method of computing averages used in the text is discussed in Appendix C.

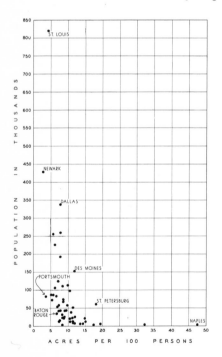

Fig. 1. Developed Areas. Acres per 100 persons.

is no fixed relationship between the total city area of a central city and its total population. Land use surveys reveal wide variations in the total land areas for cities of approximately the same populations, and point up the obvious arbitrariness of the city boundaries. Since the total city area is thus arbitrarily determined in most cases, the ratio of the total city area to a given population is not reasonable as a common denominator for comparing the land uses of one city to another. However, a definite relationship between the total *developed* area of a city and its population exists. Therefore, in this research all of the various land uses will be related to the *total developed areas.*

As the population of a city increases, less area is proportionately required for urban development. From Figure 1 it can be seen that the per capita use of land diminishes as cities become larger, until with the larger cities something of an equilibrium is reached. When the municipalities are divided into the various population groups it is interesting to note the respective percentages.

NUMBER OF CITIES	POPULATION GROUP	DEVELOPED AREA ACRES PER 100 PERSONS
28	50,000 or less	9.97
13	50,000 – 100,000	8.01
7	100,000 – 250,000	8.03
5	250,000 and over	5.04

Thus, we find in cities of less than 50,000 population significantly more land being used for all urban purposes than in the next two population groups and also almost twice as many acres per 100 persons as are utilized in cities of over 250,000 population. Further, by referring again to Figure 1 it can be seen that with few exceptions all cities tend to follow the general pattern. Thus, it can be concluded that there is a close correlation between the total amount of land used for all urban purposes and a given population.

While we will see that not all uses of land have this same relationship (for example, multifamily dwelling areas, p. 44, below), there is a tendency toward a more generous use of land in smaller cities. This is, of course, a reflection of the competition for land and the lower market value placed on a given parcel in the smaller center. Thus, to a large extent high densities are a direct result of economic pressure. The large-scale concentration of population has the effect of forcing land values up within and around an urban-

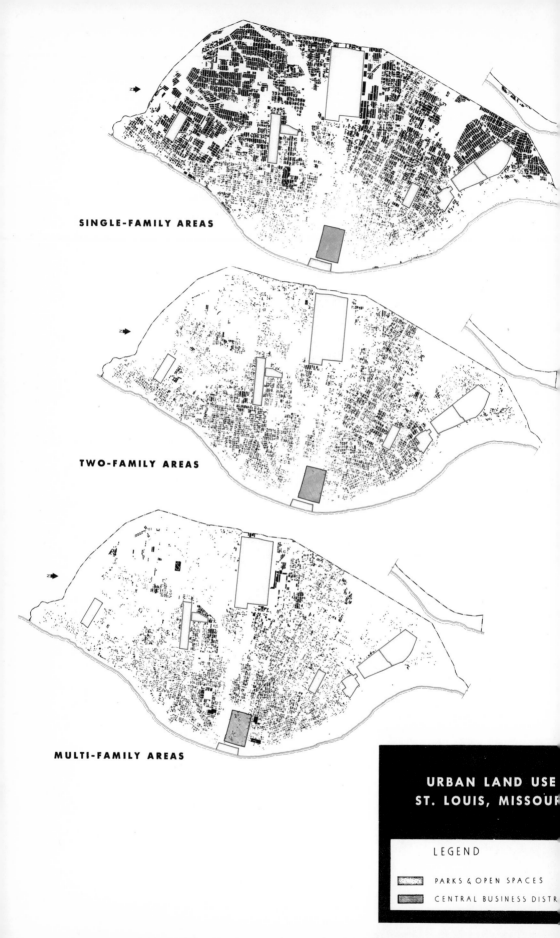

SINGLE-FAMILY AREAS

TWO-FAMILY AREAS

MULTI-FAMILY AREAS

URBAN LAND USE
ST. LOUIS, MISSOUR

LEGEND

PARKS & OPEN SPACES

CENTRAL BUSINESS DISTR

COMMERCIAL AREAS

INDUSTRIAL AND RAILROAD AREAS

VACANT AREAS

PLATE IV

ized area, reaching a peak in the core of the central city. The actual values reached vary between different cities, the general tendency being for values to increase with city size. In order to offset the handicap of high land cost in the larger city, a more intensive use is made of land by the erection of higher buildings, resulting in a denser concentration of people and use of land. This tendency will be noted with most uses; however, it will be shown that local peculiarities will often cause significant variations in the amount of land used for a particular purpose in a given community.

In addition to providing a sound basis for zoning, this study is intended to aid municipalities confronted with the problem of determining the extent of city area and the location of future boundaries. If there are definite amounts of land that can be absorbed for various purposes within a period of time, as this study will demonstrate, then it would seem desirable to determine the future extent of the city within fixed time limits. This would permit the formulation of the necessary fiscal policies to assure the establishment of utilities and services as they are needed.

The following sections of this chapter are devoted to the separate uses of urban land. A discussion of each use is presented with respect to its relationship to the total developed area of the city and to the total city population at the date of survey.

RESIDENTIAL AREAS

More of the developed area of cities is devoted to residential use than to any other use. An average of 39.61 per cent of the total developed area is so used. The proportion of the total developed area utilized by residences ranges between 20.30 per cent and 59.69 per cent; however, the vast majority of cities surveyed are within a range of between 30 and 50 per cent. Only eleven cities have percentages outside this range. The tendency for the percentage of dwelling area in a city to fall within a relatively narrow range, regardless of the size of the city, is shown in Figure 2. The few wide deviations found on this graph are those of cities having unique characteristics with specialized functions. For example, the relatively low percentage of the total developed area devoted to housing in Williamsburg, Va., is a reflection of the existence of large public areas in this historic community. At the other extreme the high residential use found in Bar Harbor, Me., is characteristic of

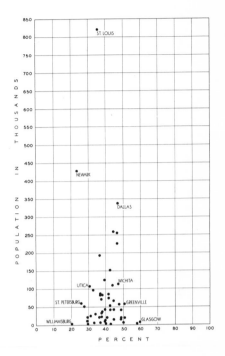

Fig. 2. Residential Areas. Percentage of total developed area.

a residential summer resort. Newark, N. J., is another striking deviation from the norm, with only 23.44 per cent of its total developed area utilized for dwelling purposes. This is due both to the high density of housing within the city and to the constrictiveness of the city boundary, which excludes much of its tributary population.

The close relationship of the dwelling area to the total developed area is illustrated by the following averages. It will be noted from this table that no significant variation exists percentagewise among the different population groups.

NUMBER OF CITIES	POPULATION GROUP	RESIDENTIAL AREA PERCENTAGE OF TOTAL DEVELOPED AREA
28	50,000 or less	39.56
13	50,000 – 100,000	37.16
7	100,000 – 250,000	41.40
5	250,000 and over	39.97

When we examine the dwelling area for relationship to population we find a strong correlation between the variables. That is, there is a marked relationship between the area absorbed for dwelling purposes and the total population of the city. Figure 3 indicates that the relationship is not a direct one since the amount of land

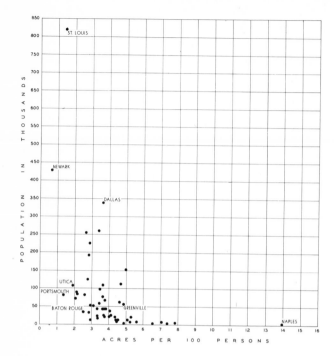

Fig. 3. Residential Areas.
Acres per 100 persons.

used is found to decrease with an increase in population. An average of 2.73 acres per 100 persons is utilized for dwelling purposes in the fifty-three central cities. Although there is a wide variation in ratios for cities with populations of less than 50,000, in the other population groups, the range found is from about 2 to 4 acres per 100 persons. The industrial centers of St. Louis, Mo., Newark, N. J., Utica, N. Y., and Portsmouth, Va., all have ratios below this range; whereas the cities of Des Moines, Iowa, Wichita, Kan., St. Petersburg, Fla., and Greenville, S. C., all possess ratios exceeding the upper limit. When all the population groups are considered, we find the trend distorted by the cities in the 100,000-250,000 population group.

NUMBER OF CITIES	POPULATION GROUP	RESIDENTIAL AREAS ACRES PER 100 PERSONS
28	50,000 or less	3.94
13	50,000 – 100,000	2.98
7	100,000 – 250,000	3.33
5	250,000 and over	2.02

Nevertheless, the trend is apparent and, in summary, it can be said that the amount of land used for dwelling areas is proportional to the total developed area of the city, and when considered as a ratio of land to population, it varies inversely with the size of the city.

Before considering the major subdivisions of residential use, it is important to recognize the local nature of the demand for housing. In each city there exists a local real estate market in which the demand for a particular type of housing structure is conditioned by factors peculiar to that community. Personal preferences as well as economic forces and social customs contribute to the variation in housing types from community to community. In combining the acreage for all types, as was done above, the local irregularities are averaged out and a more constant relationship is found between population and dwelling area. But population alone does not control the size of the dwelling areas. The density of population, intensity of land use, and size of families all enter into the total amount of land needed for dwelling purposes.

SINGLE-FAMILY DWELLING AREAS

The areas used for single-family dwellings and the distribution of these throughout the city are shown on Plate V. The cities represented were selected as typical of single-family development at different population levels.

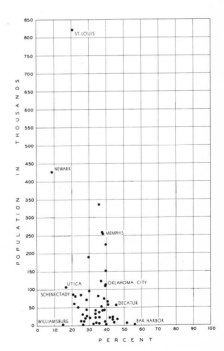

Fig. 4. Single-Family Dwellings. Percentage of total developed area.

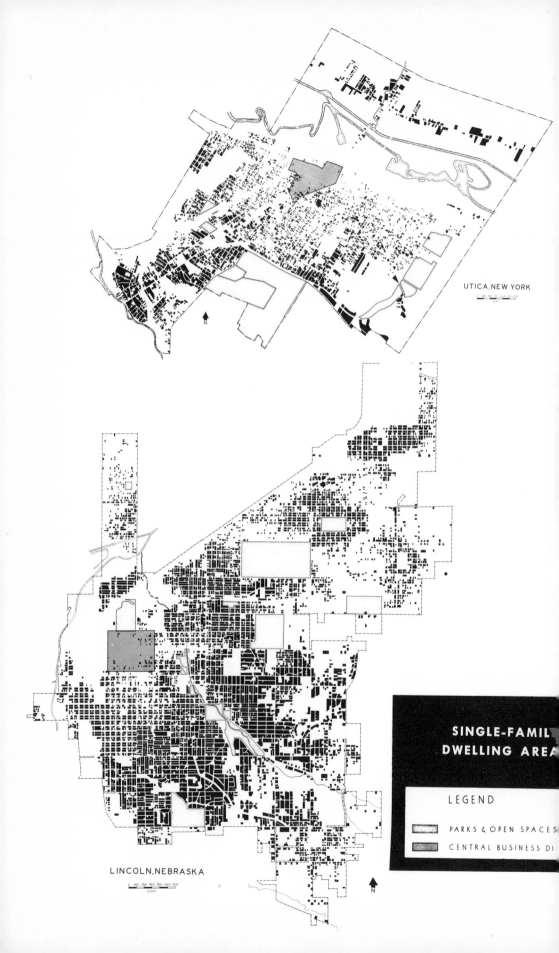

UTICA, NEW YORK

LINCOLN, NEBRASKA

SINGLE-FAMILY
DWELLING AREA

LEGEND

PARKS & OPEN SPACES

CENTRAL BUSINESS DI

WOODWARD, OKLAHOMA

0 300 600 900 1200 1500 1800'
SCALE

ST. LOUIS, MISSOURI

0 1000 2000 3000 4000 5000 6000'
SCALE

PLATE V

JACKSONVILLE, ILLINOIS

0 400 800 1200 1600 2000 2400'
SCALE

The single-family dwelling area occupies a greater percentage of the developed area of the central city than any other use, public or private. An average of 31.81 per cent of the total developed area of the city is devoted to this use. Among the smaller cities the land utilized by this subdivision of the dwelling area ranges from 15.10 per cent to 55.84 per cent, with an average of 34.08 per cent. In the next larger group of cities, those of 50,000–100,000 population, the range is narrower, being from 20.76 per cent to 45.12 per cent of the total developed area. The mean for this group is 30.92 per cent. With the exception of Utica, all the cities of between 100,000–250,000 population are within a spread of 10 per cent. The average use for all seven cities is 35.61 per cent of the total developed acreage. As might be expected in the cities of over 250,000 population, where high densities prevail, comparatively less land is devoted to single-family housing. The average found for this population group is only 28.30 per cent. The variations found among the cities surveyed are shown graphically in Figure 4 and are summarized in the following table.

NUMBER OF CITIES	POPULATION GROUP	SINGLE-FAMILY DWELLINGS PERCENTAGE OF TOTAL DEVELOPED AREA
28	50,000 or less	34.08
13	50,000 – 100,000	30.92
7	100,000 – 250,000	35.61
5	250,000 and more	28.30

The percentage of the total developed area occupied by single-family dwellings in most cities ranges between 25 and 50 per cent, while only ten of the fifty-three cities surveyed fall outside this range.* Thus, the area occupied by single-family dwellings may be counted as being reasonably constant when considered as a percentage of the total developed area.

The average number of acres per hundred persons used in central cities for single-family dwellings is 2.19. The minimum number of acres per 100 persons is 0.24 and the maximum is 12.43 for the fifty-three central cities. From Figures 4 and 5 it can be seen that the trend for single-family use has the same characteristics as that for total dwelling area. This is to be expected since the single-family area composes 80.29 per cent of the total dwelling area. The widest range in the ratio of acreage to population occurs in cities

* Only in the case of Newark, N. J., is any great deviation from the norm found. Newark has only 8.44 per cent of its total developed area in single-family use.

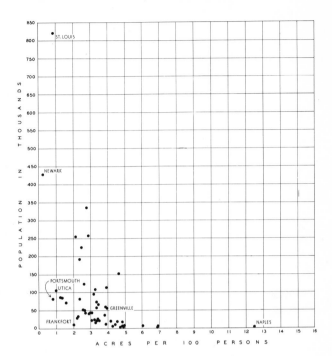

Fig. 5. Single-Family Dwellings.
Acres per 100 persons.

of less than 25,000 persons. In this group, the capital city of Frankfort, Ky., has only 1.99 acres per 100 persons, whereas the residential resort of Naples, Fla., devotes 12.43 acres per 100 to the same
use. This relatively wide range seems characteristic of smaller communities where the lack of competition for home sites permits a
more generous land use. Referring again to the graph, Figure 5, a
smaller spread is found in cities up to 100,000: 0.80 acres per 100
in the industrial center of Portsmouth, Va., to 3.90 acres in Greenville, S. C. In the group of cities in the 100,000–250,000 population
bracket there is a range of about 3.6 acres per 100 persons between
Utica, N. Y. (1.01), and Des Moines, Iowa (4.60). However, the
other five cities in the same group have a high degree of centrality
relative to the norm of 2.86 acres per 100 persons. Cities of over
250,000 population have the exceedingly low average ratio of 1.43
acres per 100 persons.

Thus, there is an apparent relationship between the population
of the city and the ratio of acreage of single-family dwelling area
to total population. When the cities are arranged in the order of
magnitude, it is seen that the largest cities have the smallest ratios.
This, of course, is expected since the single-family dwelling on a
large lot predominates in small municipalities but is not practical

in large cities. Variation of the average ratio of acres of single-family dwelling area per 100 persons in cities of different population groups is found to be as follows.

NUMBER OF CITIES	POPULATION GROUP	SINGLE-FAMILY DWELLINGS ACRES PER 100 PERSONS
28	50,000 or less	3.40
13	50,000 – 100,000	2.48
7	100,000 – 250,000	2.86
5	250,000 and over	1.43

TWO-FAMILY DWELLING AREAS

The two-family dwelling ranks second in popularity as a housing structure in central cities. However, in contrast with the large areas utilized for single-family dwellings, the two-family dwellings occupy comparatively small areas, only 4.79 per cent of the total developed area, and only 12.11 per cent of the total dwelling area of the central city.

The areas devoted to two-family dwellings in five central cities are illustrated graphically on Plate VI. These examples illustrate not only the average, but also the extremes in two-family dwelling development. Utica, N. Y., with 10.11 per cent of its total developed area occupied by two-family dwellings, is one of the cities in

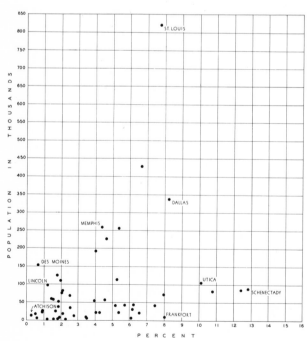

Fig. 6. Two-Family Dwellings. Percentage of total developed area.

which this form of development is most intense; Woodward, Okla., with but 0.58 per cent of its total developed area in this use, falls at the other extreme.

Two-family dwellings seldom group themselves in any particular locality. They tend to scatter through all sections of the city.* There is a tendency for the two-family dwelling to occur most often in areas of high land values, that is, close to the central business district or adjacent to major transportation arteries. The higher value of the land, together with the desire of some to live near their work, and the use of the two-family, owner-occupied dwelling as a rent-producing property, have been instrumental in sustaining the use of this type of dwelling in American cities.

In the fifty-three central cities, an average of 4.79 per cent of the total developed area is utilized for two-family dwelling purposes. The most striking feature found in comparing two-family use in the different cities is the wide variation within each of the population groups. The range among cities of less than 50,000 population is between 0.28 and 8.00 per cent of the total developed area. In the

* This scattering has often been fostered by the lack of differentiation in zoning plans between single and two-family dwellings. For example, in Toledo, O., it was only in the 1940's that a separate or exclusive one-family residence district was included in the zoning plan.

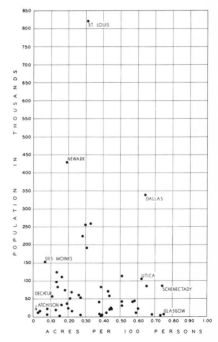

Fig. 7. Two-Family Dwellings. Acres per 100 persons.

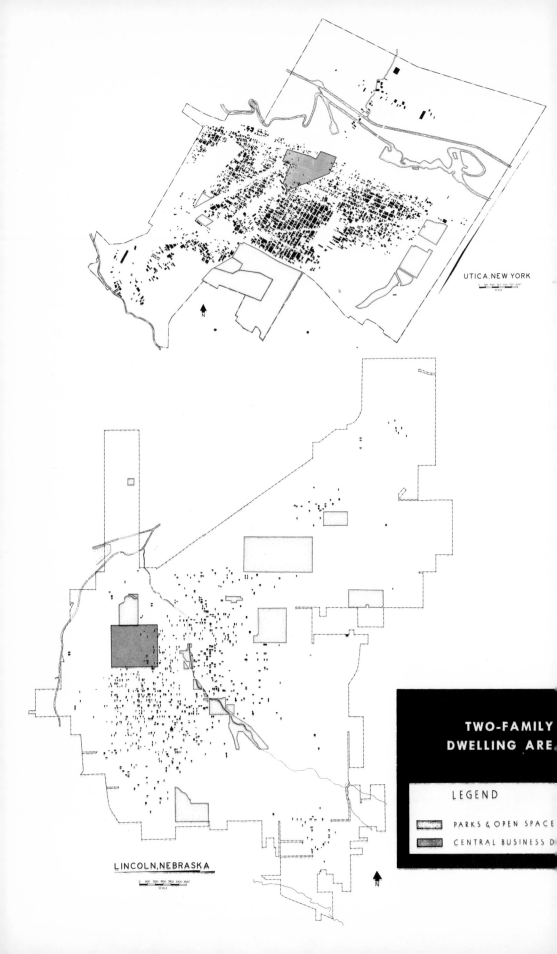

UTICA, NEW YORK

SCALE

LINCOLN, NEBRASKA

SCALE

TWO-FAMILY
DWELLING AREA

LEGEND

PARKS & OPEN SPACE
CENTRAL BUSINESS D

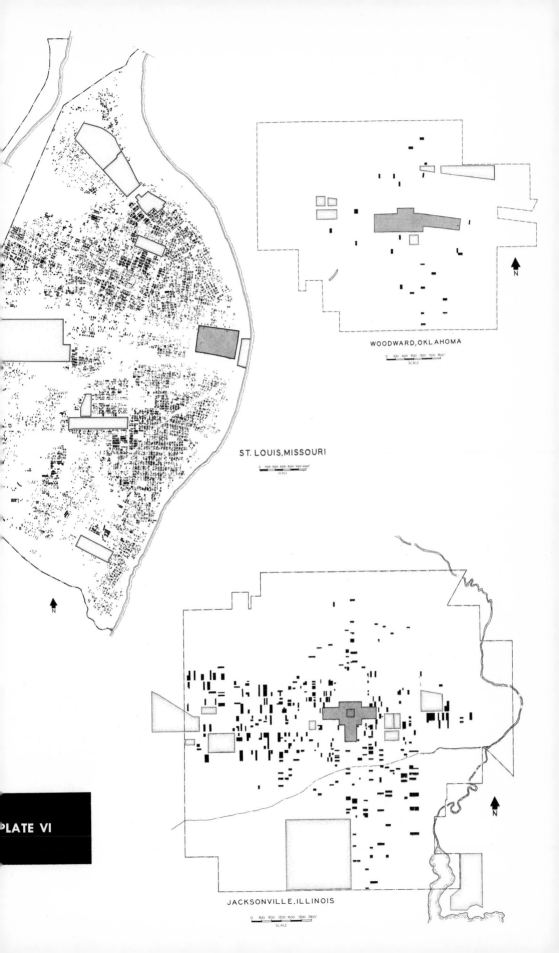

WOODWARD, OKLAHOMA

SCALE

ST. LOUIS, MISSOURI

SCALE

N

PLATE VI

JACKSONVILLE, ILLINOIS

SCALE

N

next group the range is between 1.21 per cent and 12.79 per cent of the developed area. The range found among cities of 100,000–250,000 populations is between 0.63 per cent and 10.11 per cent. The narrowest range is found among the larger cities: from 4.36 to 8.21 per cent of the total developed area. The local nature of the demand for housing was noted above, and it is in the light of local preferences and conditions that the comparative figures become most meaningful. This local preference is most clearly illustrated by the four cities ranking highest in area devoted to two-family dwellings. These cities, and the percentage of total developed area in two-family use are: Schenectady, N. Y. (12.79), Binghamton, N. Y. (12.42), Portsmouth, Va. (10.77), and Utica, N. Y. (10.11). All are eastern cities where the two-family dwelling has enjoyed traditional popularity. The deviation of these cities from the average is shown graphically in Figure 6. Summarized in the following tables are the data for the fifty-three cities.

NUMBER OF CITIES	POPULATION GROUP	TWO-FAMILY DWELLINGS PERCENTAGE OF TOTAL DEVELOPED AREA
28	50,000 or less	3.75
13	50,000 – 100,000	4.11
7	100,000 – 250,000	3.58
5	250,000 and over	6.77

The range found when the utilization is expressed as acres per 100 persons is also wide. The ratios range between 0.03 in Atchison, Kan., to 0.75 acres per 100 persons in Glasgow, Ky.—both cities of less than 13,000 population. There is an equally wide spread among the larger cities surveyed. For example, Newark, N. J., with population close to a half million, has 0.19 acres per 100 persons while Dallas, Tex., with a population of 338,000, has 0.64 acres per 100 persons devoted to this use. When the data shown in Figure 7 are divided into population groups and summarized, the following ratios are obtained.

NUMBER OF CITIES	POPULATION GROUP	TWO-FAMILY DWELLINGS ACRES PER 100 PERSONS
28	50,000 or less	0.37
13	50,000 – 100,000	0.33
7	100,000 – 250,000	0.29
5	250,000 and over	0.34

Although the two-family structure has been traditionally associated with the larger city, the increasing conversions of single-family dwellings in smaller centers is tending to change this condition. When the cities are ranked according to land use per unit of population, the following ten cities are found to have the highest ratios for two-family dwelling area:

CITY	POPULATION	TWO-FAMILY DWELLINGS ACRES PER 100 PERSONS
Glasgow, Ky.	7,040	0.75
Schenectady, N. Y.	87,549	0.74
Naples, Fla.	1,740	0.73
Marshall, Mich.	5,740	0.68
Binghamton, N. Y.	85,397	0.65
Dallas, Tex.	338,000	0.64
Utica, N. Y.	106,750	0.62
Kankakee, Ill.	22,241	0.60
Frankfort, Ky.	11,916	0.59
West Palm Beach, Fla.	44,000	0.58

Thus, there seems to be little relationship between the population and the space devoted to two-family dwellings in a community.

While the eastern cities rank highest in the percentage of their total developed area utilized by the two-family structure, this regional variation is not found when the ratio of dwelling area to population is considered. Therefore it may be assumed that while the actual number of two-family units in cities of the Middle West is relatively large, they occupy small sites.

The future popularity of the two-family dwelling cannot be determined with any accuracy. There has been an overall decrease in the number of two-family dwellings built since the 1920's. Within the past ten years about 4 per cent of all dwelling units started have been two-family units. The demand for the two-family unit continued following World War II, when much of the market was met through conversions of existing structures. However, this was a period when residential construction was affected by an acute shortage of dwelling units. It is safe to assume that many of the new two-family units were provided in response to this unusual market condition.

Despite the wide variations found in the space given over to two-family dwellings in the different cities surveyed, it appears that the total amount of area used for two-family dwellings will always be rather small. Although the area utilized is sometimes over 10 per cent of the total developed area of the city, in the majority of cases it does not exceed 5 per cent.

MULTIFAMILY DWELLING AREAS

With the rising standard of living for a large part of the urban population during the first decades of this century, many people forsook the congested tenement for more spacious or efficient quarters. While many of these families found modest houses, others without the desire or without the economic means to command a single-family house found accommodations in apartments. The apartment has become popular in areas of high land values for both the married and unmarried, and for families with or without children, in spite of its deficiencies for some of these groups.

The multifamily dwelling reached its peak of popularity in 1928 when 39 per cent of all urban dwelling units started were of this type. Relatively few units were started during the 1930's. However, since the end of World War II, with the revival of the housing market, stimulated by government credit assistance, there has been a rebirth of their popularity. Although there has been a decline in the number of new units started since the peak years of 1948–1949, over 12 per cent of all new urban dwelling units started in 1952 were of the multifamily type.*

The distribution of the multifamily dwelling area in five representative cities is shown on Plate VII. The acceptance of the apartment as a living unit by various income groups has tended to scatter apartment houses throughout the city. In general multifamily structures have tended to predominate in the "zone of transition" adjacent to the central business district, in the immediate vicinity of commercial subcenters, and along arterial thoroughfares. In this respect they resemble the two-family dwellings; greater numbers occur close to the central area and they become fewer as the city limits are approached. However, this pattern is changing somewhat. In some suburban areas, particularly industrial satellites, apartment houses are conspicuously present although, on the whole, developments in fringe areas have in the past been largely single-family dwellings. Large-scale projects insured by the Federal Housing Authority and requiring large areas of land, usually available only in the fringe areas of most cities, are changing this pattern. There tend to be larger concentrations of apartment units, often a single project covering several blocks, in what have by tradition been single-family dwelling areas.

* Housing and Home Finance Agency (Washington, D. C.) bulletin, *Housing Statistics* (January 1953), p. 3.

Of the total dwelling area in fifty-three cities, 7.60 per cent is devoted to multifamily dwellings. This land accounts for an average of 3.01 per cent of the total developed area of these central cities. The range found among the fifty-three cities surveyed was less than 7 per cent: Atchison, Kan., with only 0.46 per cent of its total developed area in this use formed the minimum, and Newark, N. J., with 8.34 per cent, the maximum.

When each population group is studied, it is found that there is a distinct tendency for the percentage of land used for multifamily dwellings to increase with an increase in population. The following table points up this tendency.

NUMBER OF CITIES	POPULATION GROUP	MULTIFAMILY DWELLINGS PERCENTAGE OF TOTAL DEVELOPED AREA
28	50,000 or less	1.73
13	50,000 – 100,000	2.13
7	100,000 – 250,000	2.21
5	250,000 and over	4.90

The dispersion of the percentages for the individual cities around the group average is shown graphically in Figure 8.

The average area used for multifamily dwellings per 100 persons for the fifty-three central cities is 0.21 acres, although the ratios

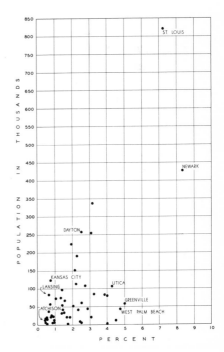

Fig. 8. Multifamily Dwellings. Percentage of total developed area.

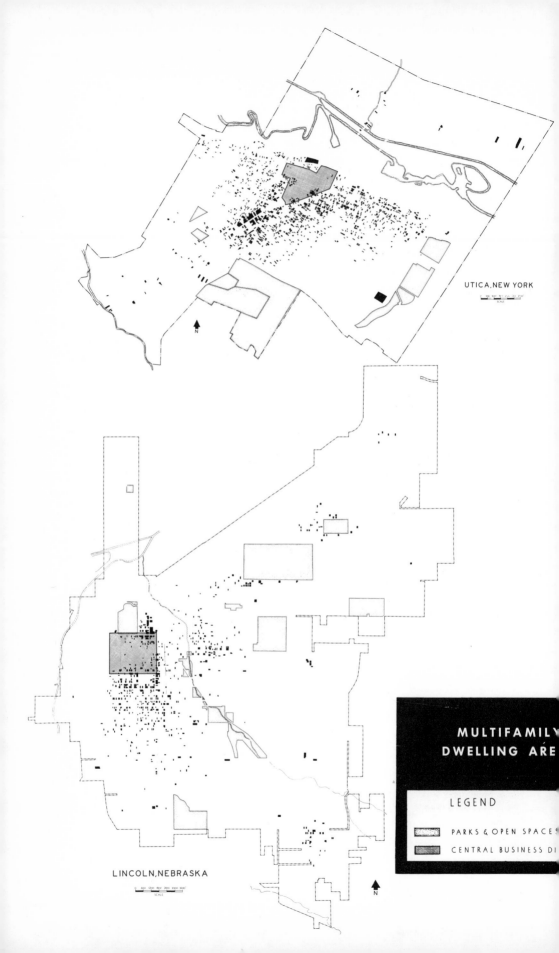

UTICA, NEW YORK

N

LINCOLN, NEBRASKA

N

MULTIFAMILY
DWELLING ARE

LEGEND

PARKS & OPEN SPACE

CENTRAL BUSINESS DI

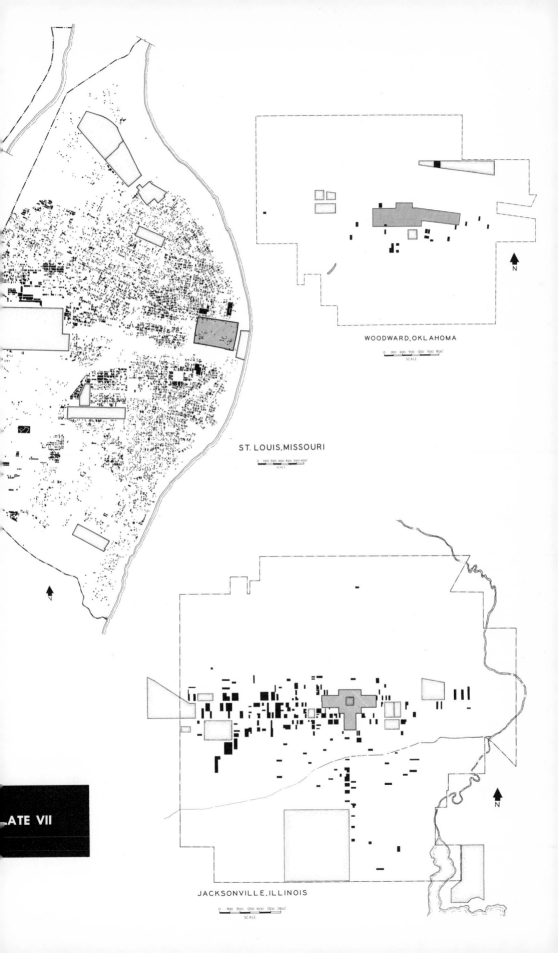

WOODWARD, OKLAHOMA

SCALE

ST. LOUIS, MISSOURI

SCALE

PLATE VII

JACKSONVILLE, ILLINOIS

SCALE

for individual cities vary from 0.04 to 1.29 acres per 100 persons. However, all but five of the fifty-three cities studied have ratios of less than 0.40 acres per 100 persons. The graphic dispersion of the ratios for the fifty-three cities is shown in Figure 9.

There is an apparent relationship between the size of the city and the area per population used for multifamily buildings. Unlike the case of the single-family dwelling area where the ratio diminishes as the population increases, in multifamily use it is found that the larger the city the greater the ratio of this land use to population. Placing the cities in their population groups the following ratios are found.

NUMBER OF CITIES	POPULATION GROUP	MULTIFAMILY DWELLINGS ACRES PER 100 PERSONS
28	50,000 or less	0.17
13	50,000 – 100,000	0.17
7	100,000 – 250,000	0.18
5	250,000 and over	0.25

Although the ratio for the first two population groups closely approximates that of the third group, it will be noted from Figure 9 that the five cities deviating radically from the norm lie in these lower groups, thus causing undue distortion. The cities are: Wil-

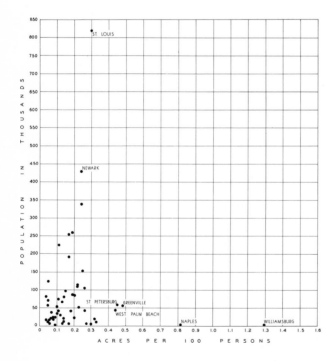

Fig. 9. Multifamily Dwellings.
Acres per 100 persons.

liamsburg, Va. (1.29), Naples, Fla. (0.81), Greenville, C. C. (0.48), St. Petersburg, Fla. (0.45), and West Palm Beach, Fla. (0.44). If these few extremes were not included, the average ratios of the first two groups would be lower, and the increasing ratio with the increase in city size would be even more apparent.

In summary, the future use of the multifamily dwelling is not predictable with any degree of certainty. Local preference, as well as the extent of federal participation in insuring mortgages on this property, will in a large part determine the rate of construction of this type of unit. Despite the spectacular demand for apartment units in the postwar period, if the American family has the economic means it is reasonable to assume a greater trend toward home ownership and away from the apartment.* There are many factors which will sustain the multifamily dwelling as a prominent feature of urban housing. Among these are the high value of land in large centers, the transient nature of a large part of the population, the rise of the "efficiency" and the "de luxe" apartment, the existence of a part of the population unable or unwilling to accept the fixed financial burdens of home ownership, and the general acceptance of the apartment as a means of housing in the city. It is improbable, judging from the data studied, that large areas will ever be absorbed for this use. It follows that overgenerous zoning of areas for multifamily dwelling use is unnecessary and unwise and in itself encouraging to speculation in the land market.

SUMMARY OF RESIDENTIAL USES

When all three of the residential classifications are combined, a better understanding of their relative proportions is realized. The following table shows part of this summary which emphasizes the importance of residential areas, and especially single-family dwellings, in the general pattern of urban land uses.

Residential areas in the fifty-three central cities occupy almost 40 per cent of the total developed area. Single-family dwellings account for 80.29 per cent, or about four-fifths of the total residential area. This is over six times the amount of two-family development, and almost eleven times that of multifamily dwellings.

---

* This does not overlook the large number of apartment houses being constructed under government sponsorship. Should government policy continue to support construction of low-density multifamily housing, it may be necessary to restudy future land use in light of this trend.

TYPE OF USE	FIFTY-THREE CITIES: PERCENTAGE OF TOTAL DEVELOPED AREA	FIFTY-THREE CITIES PERCENTAGE OF TOTAL RESIDENTIAL AREA
Single-family dwellings	31.81	80.29
Two-family dwellings	4.79	12.11
Multifamily dwellings	3.01	7.60
Total residential	39.61	100.00

While residential areas compose almost 40 per cent of the total developed area, they become even more significant when expressed as a percentage of privately developed property. Residential uses, as found in the fifty-three central cities, occupy 80.23 per cent or four-fifths of all land privately developed.

We now turn to the use of land for nonresidential purposes—purposes that utilize 60.39 per cent of the total developed area of the city.

COMMERCIAL AREAS

The demand for land for commercial activities is related to the business profits anticipated from its use. The competition for the most advantageous sites places a higher market value on commercial land than can be commanded by most other uses of urban land. Consequently, during the period of rapid expansion of our cities, when there was a spectacular growth of commercial establishments, all land in the daily stream of community activities was optimistically viewed as potential commercial property. The strip along each major thoroughfare, the corners of every busy street intersection, and a large zone centering on the hub of the city were seen as choice business sites. This overexploitation of land was fostered by numerous individuals and groups interested in quick turnovers and high returns. Moreover, without an adequate measure of the relationship between commercial uses and the population to be served, early zoning plans were generally forced to recognize this speculative urge in order to secure adoption.

Although pressure for too liberal business zoning still comes from some misguided or overoptimistic property owners, it has long been evident that there is an optimum amount of space that can be absorbed by commercial uses for a given population. The overzoning of business land is detrimental in many ways. First, it has created this surplus commercial supply on the erroneous assumption that it would ultimately be used. This has depressed property values for owners in the less strategic locations. In turn this has weakened the tax structure of the city. But equally important, overzoning has the effect of sterilizing large areas that otherwise might have been developed for some other use. Land so zoned has been spottily developed with single-family or other "higher type" uses, and so the zoning plan neither recognizes the existence of many homes in the area nor gives sufficient protection to the strategic locations for which there is a genuine commercial demand. In sum, overzoning tends to sterilize ribbon frontage areas for any effective use, and the proper land is not reserved for the vital needs of commerce.

The average amount of land used for commercial purposes in fifty-three cities is 3.32 per cent of the total developed area. When the cities are arranged by population groups the following averages are obtained.

NUMBER OF CITIES	POPULATION GROUP	COMMERCIAL AREAS PERCENTAGE OF TOTAL DEVELOPED AREA
28	50,000 or less	3.14
13	50,000 – 100,000	2.58
7	100,000 – 250,000	2.90
5	250,000 and over	4.26

From this data can be seen a trend. The percentage of area devoted to commerce increases as the size of the city increases. The average amount of land used for this purpose in cities of less than 50,000 is greater than in either of the next two population groups. However, by reference to Figure 10 it can be seen that all but five cities with populations of less than 50,000 lie within a range of less than 2 per cent. Cities outside this range include the tourist centers of Williamsburg, Va., Naples, Fla., Bar Harbor, Me., and West Palm Beach, Fla. In each of these cases a higher than normal amount of retail space would be expected. The ranges in the next two population groups are relatively narrow and the averages for each are correspondingly close (2.58 and 2.90 per cent respectively). In cities of over 250,000 the percentage of the total developed area occupied by commerce is materially greater (4.26) than that recorded for any of the other groups. The range for these five larger cities is wide, with extremes of 2.33 per cent for Dallas, Tex., and 6.39 per cent for Newark, N. J.

An examination of figures for the acres of commercial develop-

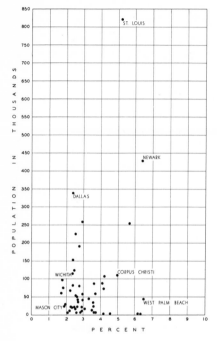

Fig. 10. Commercial Areas. Percentage of total developed area.

ment per 100 persons shows that there is little variation between the ratios of the different population groups.

NUMBER OF CITIES	POPULATION GROUP	COMMERCIAL AREAS ACRES PER 100 PERSONS
28	50,000 or less	0.31
13	50,000 – 100,000	0.21
7	100,000 – 250,000	0.23
5	250,000 and over	0.21

While the three larger population groups have averages equal to or just less than the average for the fifty-three cities, which is 0.23 per cent, there is a significant difference in the average for the group of cities of less than 50,000 population. From Figure 11 it will be seen that for the individual cities, the widest range in ratio is in this lower group—a range of from 0.14 acres for Petersburg, Va., to 2.99 acres per 100 persons in Naples, Fla.

There are a number of factors that influence the amount of space required by commerce and that tend to account for this variation among cities. The wide spread of ratios among the smaller cities is due substantially to the character of the city: both cities having high ratios (Naples and Williamsburg) are communities providing mainly retail services to transient or seasonal populations. The density of population is another factor. Where the popu-

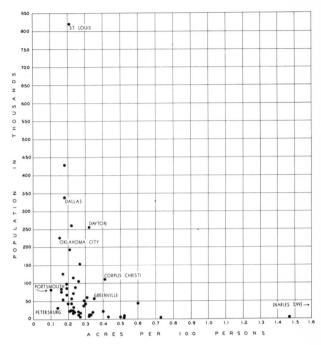

**Fig. 11. Commercial Areas.
Acres per 100 persons.**

lation is concentrated, and thus travel distances are shorter, fewer stores are needed to serve the people. In the smaller cities commercial facilities are almost entirely confined to a single area in the center of town. Another factor is the trading area. For example, although Tuscola, Ill., is a city of less than 3,000 population, it has almost three-fourths of an acre of commercial development per 100 persons, for Tuscola serves as the primary trading center for an agricultural district. To carry this point further, it is apparent that in the case of smaller cities, the proximity of larger centers reduces the need for commercial outlets in the smaller outlying city. The small shopping centers found in the suburbs are patent examples. The economic and social characteristics of a community are perhaps equally important factors since the demand for commercial outlets depends very largely on the income levels (and values) in the community.

It is difficult to measure the importance of each of these factors, but it can be said that although small cities have a proportionately greater area devoted to commercial enterprises than larger cities, the size of the commercial area cannot be directly related to the population because of the important influence of local characteristics in individual cities.

49

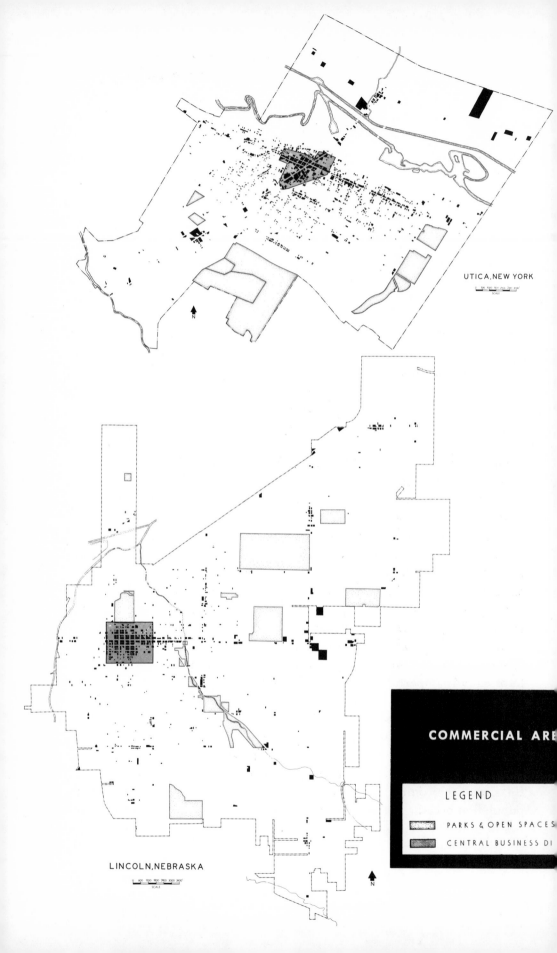

UTICA, NEW YORK

SCALE

LINCOLN, NEBRASKA

SCALE

COMMERCIAL ARE

LEGEND

PARKS & OPEN SPACES

CENTRAL BUSINESS DI

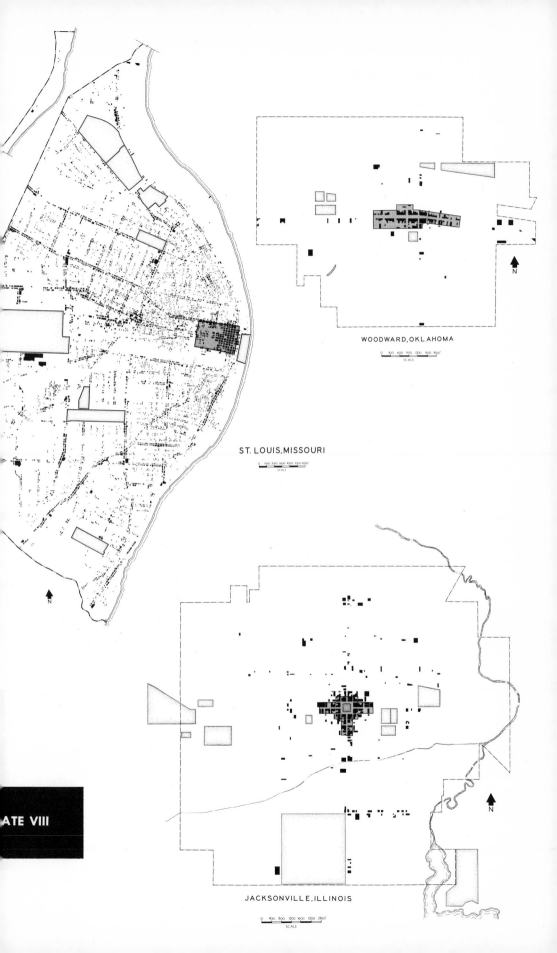

WOODWARD, OKLAHOMA

0 300 600 900 1200 1500 1800
SCALE

ST. LOUIS, MISSOURI

0 1000 2000 3000 4000 5000 6000
SCALE

N

N

ATE VIII

JACKSONVILLE, ILLINOIS

0 400 800 1200 1600 2000 2400
SCALE

N

Although the area necessary for the total commercial development is only 1.70 to 6.49 per cent of the total developed area, the average city has seldom realistically apportioned the area needed to serve future requirements.* The present areas used for commercial purposes in five cities are indicated on Plate VIII. The cities shown have commercial developments typical of those encountered in central cities.

The commercial development in the central business district stands out clearly in all of these cities. With few exceptions the central retail district is found at the center of all transportation channels, although this location may not be the geographic center of the city. But not all of the commercial use is found within this core area. First, business uses diminish with increases in distance from the central area. Secondly, there is a radial dispersion of uses abutting and stretching out along major traffic arteries, although this development is by no means solid or continuous. It will be seen that at important street intersections this development forms a cluster. In some cases these nucleations have become outlying business centers. However, such occurrences are more often found in larger cities.

LIGHT INDUSTRY

The light industrial area of central cities has in the past centered on the main business district of the city. This area sometimes surrounds the business core, but most often is to one side or another of the major commercial concentration. The area itself is a zone of transition containing a variety of land uses ranging from heavy manufacturing to residence. While some of these uses are out of place, others are not; for example, wholesale trade and light storage are complementary to the central business district. In addition, many smaller manufacturing establishments such as those engaged in printing, garment production, and jewelry manufacture have sought this central position for their plants. While some light industry has been located in peripheral areas to gain larger sites, there are still strong ties between certain light manufacturing processes and the central area.

The amount of land devoted to light industrial use varies in

* For example, in Jefferson City, Mo., only 22 per cent of the area presently zoned for commerce is so utilized.

accordance with the character of the city and its tributary region. This use accounts for an average of 2.84 per cent of the total developed area of the central cities, although a range of between 0.35 and 7.26 per cent is found for the fifty-three cities surveyed.

From Figure 12 it is seen that the wide variations in use found between the different cities is not confined to any one population group although the range is somewhat narrow in the larger cities. Thus, as in the cases of most uses of urban land, wider variation may be expected among a group of small cities. A range of 0.35–7.26 is found for the twenty-eight cities with populations of less than 50,000. The other cities, arranged in ascending population groups, have ranges of 0.59–5.11, 1.29–4.33, and 1.47–6.58 respectively.

The average amount of land utilized by light industry, expressed as a percentage of the total developed area, is as follows.

NUMBER OF CITIES	POPULATION GROUP	LIGHT INDUSTRY PERCENTAGE OF TOTAL DEVELOPED AREA
28	50,000 or less	2.78
13	50,000 – 100,000	2.09
7	100,000 – 250,000	2.36
5	250,000 and over	3.76

The ratio of the acreage used for light industry to the given pop-

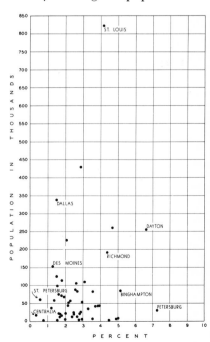

Fig. 12. Light Industry. Percentage of total developed area.

ulation unit of 100 persons varies between 0.03 and 0.60 acres. The average utilization found for the fifty-three central cities is 0.20 acres. The greatest range in ratio is found in cities of less than 50,000. Centralia, Ill., a city in this group, has only 0.03 acres compared to the 0.60 acres per 100 persons utilized in Petersburg, Va. In the three larger population groups the range between cities is narrower. Racine, Wis., has the lowest ratio of all cities of 50,000–100,000 population, whereas Binghamton, N. Y., has the highest: respectively, 0.09 acres and 0.27 acres per 100 persons. In the next group Kansas City, Kan., has the lowest ratio with 0.11 acres per 100 persons and Richmond, Va., with 0.34 acres, the highest. Among the large cities Newark, N. J., has the low ratio of 0.08 acres per 100 persons in Dayton, Ohio, with 0.37 acres, the high ratio.

The ratios for the individual cities are shown graphically in Figure 13. When we consider only the averages for each population group, a considerable similarity of ratios is found.

NUMBER OF CITIES	POPULATION GROUP	LIGHT INDUSTRY ACRES PER 100 PERSONS
28	50,000 or less	0.28
13	50,000 – 100,000	0.17
7	100,000 – 250,000	0.19
5	250,000 and over	0.19

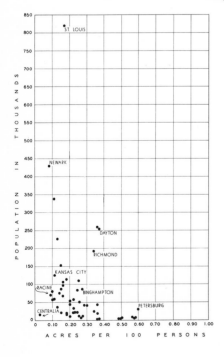

Fig. 13. Light Industry. Acres per 100 persons.

Here, again, is found a more liberal use of land in the smaller cities. Cities of less than 50,000 population use on an average a third more land per unit of population than larger cities.

In summary, while the amount of land area in a community devoted to light industry varies widely from community to community, there seems to be a relationship between the percentage of land absorbed for this use and the population in cities of more than 50,000 people. For cities of smaller size, however, there is no apparent relationship.

In a large part, light industrial uses are local in nature. They are service establishments—laundries, garages, wholesale firms, small printing plants, etc.—that cater to the city and its environs. Because of this, we may expect to find a closer relationship between the acreage used and the population served than is the case with heavy industries that are not oriented to a local market.

HEAVY INDUSTRY

The location of heavy industry in any municipality depends upon factors that are economic in nature, and that are local as well as national in scope. Chief among these are availability of the materials of manufacture, sources of power, communications, and transportation, and of people—both employees and consumers.

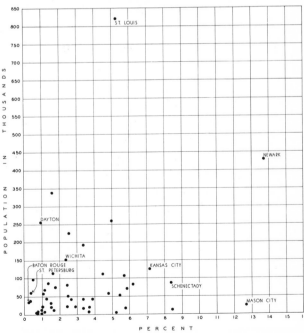

Fig. 14. Heavy Industry. Percentage of total developed area.

Slightly more urban land is used by heavy industry than by light industry. Summaries of the data for fifty-three central cities reveal that 3.60 per cent of the total developed area is occupied by heavy industry as compared with 2.84 per cent occupied by light industry. Appreciably more land is devoted to heavy industry in the larger cities—an average of 4.70 per cent of the total developed area of the cities with population ranging over 250,000 is so used as compared with 2.87, 2.70, and 3.48 per cent found in other size groups (see Figure 14).

NUMBER OF CITIES	POPULATION GROUP	HEAVY INDUSTRY PERCENTAGE OF TOTAL DEVELOPED AREA
28	50,000 or less	2.87
13	50,000 – 100,000	2.70
7	100,000 – 250,000	3.48
5	250,000 and over	4.70

Wider variations in the ratios of land use to population are evident in heavy industrial use than in light industrial use. Two of the central cities surveyed, Bar Harbor, Me., and Santa Fe, N. M., were devoid of heavy industry. The range found for the remaining cities varied between 0.01 and 1.50 acres per 100 persons.

The average use for heavy industry per population unit for the central cities is 0.25 acres. Both extremes for the fifty-three cities (0.01 and 1.50 acres per 100 persons) are found among the cities of less than 50,000 population. The unusually low ratio of 0.01 acres belongs to Baton Rouge, La., whose major industries are located beyond the corporate limits. In cities of 50,000–100,000 persons we find a smaller range of ratios. Of this group, Lincoln, Neb., has the low ratio of 0.05 acres per 100 persons. Contrasted with the governmental center of Lincoln, the important manufacturing center of Schenectady, N. Y., has a ratio of 0.48 acres per 100 persons. Oklahoma City, Okla., and Wichita, Kan., have identical ratios of 0.16 acres per 100 persons which represents the low extreme found in cities of 100,000–250,000 population. At the other extreme in this group, Kansas City, Kan., devotes 0.51 acres per 100 persons to heavy industry. In the largest cities—those with populations over 250,000—Dayton, Ohio, utilizes only 0.05 acres per 100 persons for heavy industry. Although Dayton is known as a manufacturing center, some of its largest industries occupy relatively small properties while others are outside the corporate limits. Newark, N. J., with a ratio of 0.40 acres, is high for this group. The average use by population groups is as follows.

NUMBER OF CITIES	POPULATION GROUP	HEAVY INDUSTRY ACRES PER 100 PERSONS
28	50,000 or less	0.29
13	50,000 – 100,000	0.21
7	100,000 – 250,000	0.28
5	250,000 and over	0.24

While these averages would seem to indicate a rather constant relationship between the area used by industry and a given population, such is not the case. From Figure 15 it can be seen that there is little if any relationship between these two variables. The individuality of a given city is more pronounced in the absorption of land for heavy industry than for light industry. The concentration of industry in a particular city is, of course, largely dependent upon economic factors. While some light industry processes and services are essential in any community, heavy industry often serves a regional or national market rather than a local area. Thus, in many cases cities of a relatively large size have not attracted heavy industry, or if they have, industry has located outside the city where large sites are available at lower costs. There are rare cases (con-

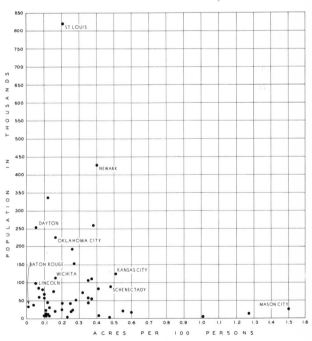

Fig. 15. Heavy Industry.
Acres per 100 persons.

fined to relatively small cities) in which no heavy industry is found within the city at all.

RAILROAD PROPERTY

The amount of land given over to railroad property varies from community to community according to each city's economic function and its position in the transportation network. Fifty-two of the cities under discussion have railroads within their city boundaries, Bar Harbor, Me., being the exception. The average amount of railroad area for these cities is 4.86 per cent of the total developed area.

		RAILROAD PROPERTY	
NUMBER OF CITIES	POPULATION GROUP	PERCENTAGE OF TOTAL DEVELOPED AREA	ACRES PER 100 PERSONS
28	50,000 or less	4.99	0.50
13	50,000 – 100,000	4.85	0.39
7	100,000 – 250,000	5.39	0.43
5	250,000 and over	4.38	0.22

As might be expected the amount of land devoted to railroad usage varies considerably between cities and with little regard to population (see Table 2 and Figure 16). Cities that are transfer points on the national rail system or terminals for regional lines have,

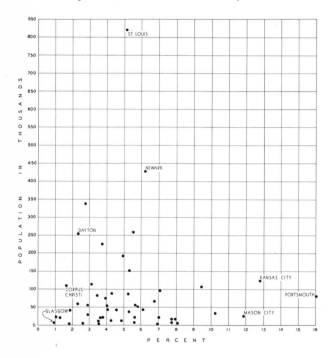

Fig. 16. Railroad Property. Percentage of total developed area.

of course, large areas for this use. Portsmouth, Va. (16.16 per cent) and Kansas City, Kan. (12.76 per cent) are cases in point. Furthermore, small cities on transcontinental lines may have relatively large areas absorbed by this use. Woodward, Okla., a city of some 6000 persons, has 8.08 per cent of its total developed area in railroad property. On an average, railroad property occupies a larger pecentage of a city's developed area than either light or heavy industry, but occupies about three-fourths as much as the total area of light and heavy industry combined.

COMBINED LIGHT AND HEAVY INDUSTRY AND RAILROADS

Railroad property falls under the broad classification of publicly developed land. However, because of its fundamental tie with industry and its juxtaposition to industrial areas, it has been combined with the industrial property for a special analysis. The following table shows data for the combined uses.

| | | COMBINED INDUSTRY AND RAILROAD PROPERTY | |
NUMBER OF CITIES	POPULATION GROUP	PERCENTAGE OF TOTAL DEVELOPED AREA	ACRES PER 100 PERSONS
28	50,000 or less	10.64	1.07
13	50,000 – 100,000	9.64	0.77
7	100,000 – 250,000	11.23	0.90
5	250,000 and over	12.84	0.65

The size of a city does not appear to affect the general ratio between the combined industrial and railroad uses and the total developed area. The four population groups do not vary greatly from the overall average of 11.30 per cent. The area per population occupied by these combined uses also shows no consistent relationship to the total city population.

An examination of the individual city percentages reveals a wide range indicating that the relative proportion of industry and railroads to the total developed area varies according to each city's particular characteristics. Forty-three of the fifty-three central cities have combined percentages within the relatively wide range of from 6.00 to 16.00 per cent. See Figure 17. The amount of land per population unit devoted to these combined uses is shown graphically in Figure 18.

The area in combined industrial and railroad development in five central cities is shown on Plate IX. Except for small-scale oper-

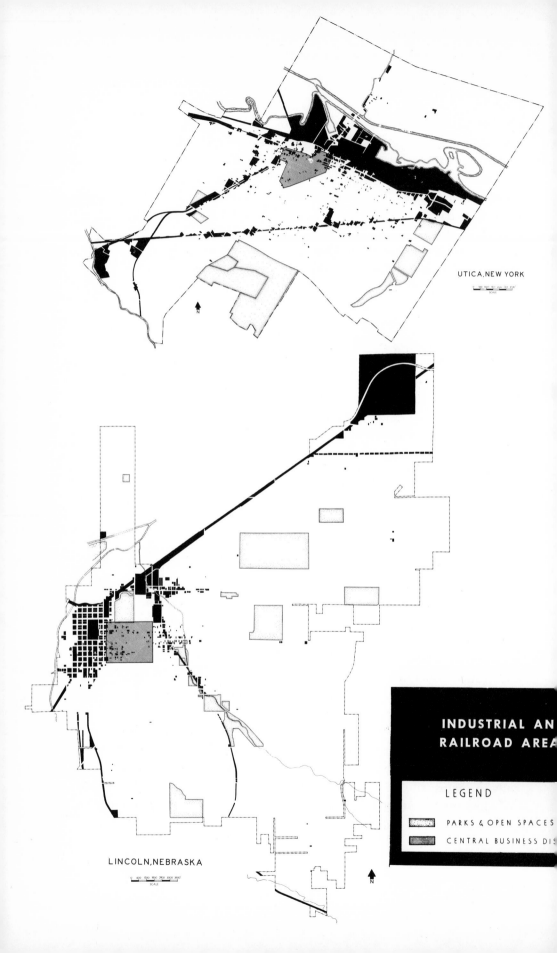

UTICA, NEW YORK

LINCOLN, NEBRASKA

INDUSTRIAL AN
RAILROAD AREA

LEGEND

PARKS & OPEN SPACES
CENTRAL BUSINESS DIS

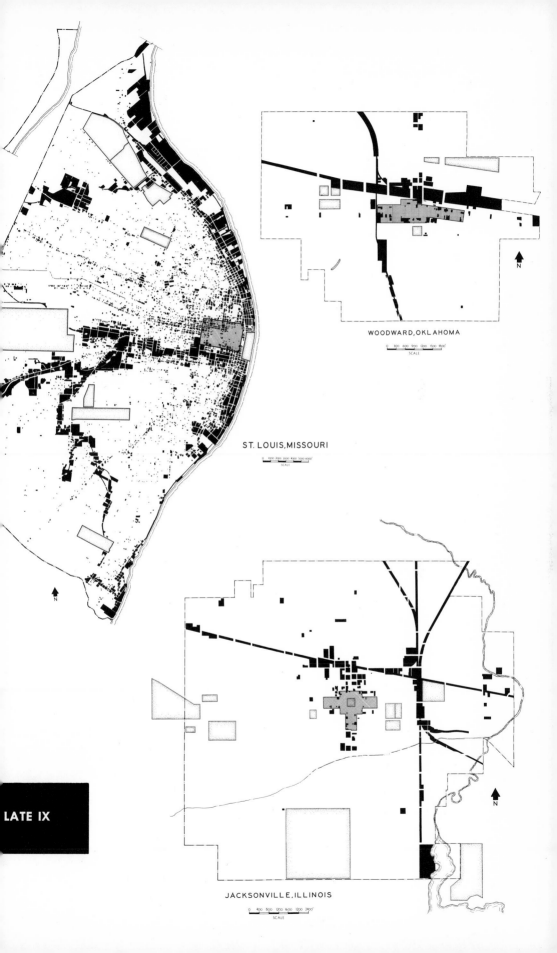

WOODWARD, OKLAHOMA

ST. LOUIS, MISSOURI

LATE IX

JACKSONVILLE, ILLINOIS

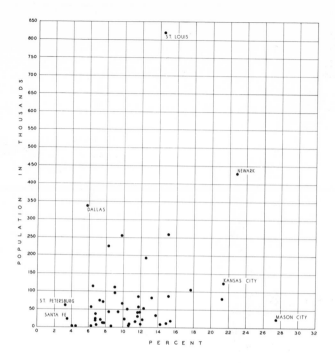

Fig. 17. Combined Light and
Heavy Industry and
Railroad Property.
Percentage of total
developed area.

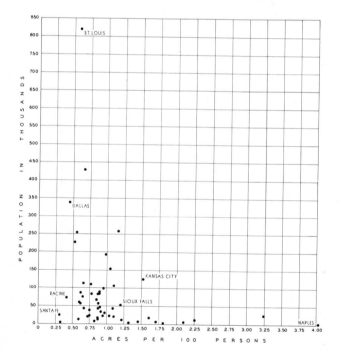

Fig. 18. Combined Light and
Heavy Industry and
Railroad Property. Acres
per 100 persons.

ations involving materials and products that are easily handled, many manufacturing and service establishments require rail connections. Although some of these industries can be adequately served by motor transportation, one of the prime requisites for industrial location is access to main-line rail service. Thus, we find that the major industrial areas tend to cling to railroad routes. There are exceptions, of course. Some older manufacturers of the lighter types have been located independent to direct rail service and have depended upon motor transportation. Also, newer industries that can operate effectively without rail service have developed in peripheral areas. Nevertheless, heavy industry processing bulk materials and handling heavy products will continue to depend on rail transportation. Since heavy industries occupy a large percentage of all industrial land, it follows that the bulk of industry will be found close to railroad transportation.

STREETS

The second largest use of urban land is that area occupied by streets, alleys, highways, and boulevards—land devoted solely to providing access to other urban land and development. All types of public and private vehicle traffic rights-of-way that provide this accessibility are summarized as "streets." On the average, 28.10 per cent of the developed area of the central city is devoted to streets.

NUMBER OF CITIES	POPULATION GROUP	STREETS PERCENTAGE OF TOTAL DEVELOPED AREA
28	50,000 or less	28.33
13	50,000 – 100,000	33.27
7	100,000 – 250,000	27.57
5	250,000 and over	24.75

This summary shows a relatively constant relationship between street area and the total developed area, as would be expected. Over two-thirds of all cities surveyed have street areas within the range of 23 to 35 per cent of the total developed area, with over two-fifths falling within a range of 25 to 30 per cent. See Figure 19. The most notable exception to all this is St. Petersburg, Fla., with over 55 per cent of its developed area in streets. This is a result of the excessive land subdivision of a "boom" period.

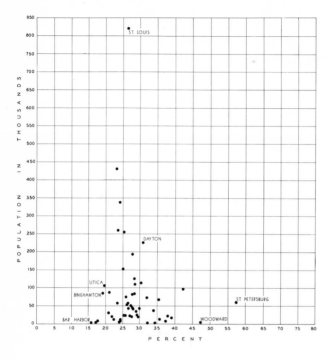

Fig. 19. Streets. Percentage of
total developed area.

Smaller cities tend to have more street area per unit of population than do larger cities with their more intensive residential development.

NUMBER OF CITIES	POPULATION GROUP	STREETS ACRES PER 100 PERSONS
28	50,000 or less	2.82
13	50,000 – 100,000	2.66
7	100,000 – 250,000	2.21
5	250,000 and over	1.25

This tendency is clearly seen in the averages above. Cities of less than 100,000 population, on an average, utilize over twice as much land for streets in proportion to population as do the cities of 250,000 and over. The ratios for the individual cities are shown graphically in Figure 20.

In summary, the amount of space devoted to streets varies according to the characteristics of individual cities, although there is a fairly constant ratio of land so used to population. Varying standards for street widths, prevailing policies of land subdivision control, and the density of development are all factors in the use of land for streets. More important, perhaps, is the fact that the characteristic street pattern of all cities surveyed is the "gridiron." This rigid pattern of street development requires appreciably more land to pro-

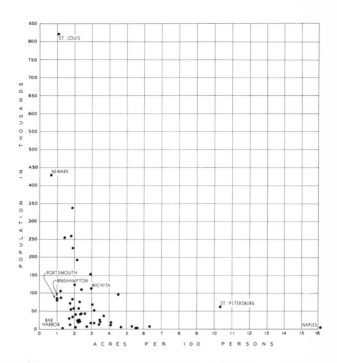

Fig. 20. Streets. Acres per 100 persons.

vide the same service than is required by street systems based on functional and informal design principles. Newer methods of sub-division design, particularly where there are fewer and larger blocks, will result in lower ratios. Plans which differentiate between heavy traffic thoroughfares and access roads also reduce land requirements for streets.

PARKS AND PLAYGROUNDS

Parks and playgrounds constitute an average of nearly 7.00 per cent of the developed area of central cities, with a range among cities from 0.17 to 20.87 per cent. Excluding Bar Harbor, Me., which has no park land within its boundaries, we find that Glasgow, Ky., possesses the low ratio of 0.17 per cent while Petersburg, Va., has the high extreme of 20.87 per cent. Both cities have populations of less than 50,000. The averages for each of the population groups follow.

NUMBER OF CITIES	POPULATION GROUP	PARKS AND PLAYGROUNDS PERCENTAGE OF TOTAL DEVELOPED AREA
28	50,000 or less	5.08
13	50,000 – 100,000	6.53
7	100,000 – 250,000	5.68
5	250,000 and over	8.59

There is a tendency, as this table indicates, for the percentage of total developed land allocated to parks and playgrounds to increase with the population. From Figure 21 it can be seen that cities of less than 50,000 population often have a relatively small percentage of the developed area in park use: half of all the cities in this group have less than 3.00 per cent of the developed area in this use. Although the two extremes are found in the smallest population groups, a wide range is also found in the others. In the case of the larger cities, it can be seen, however, that the individual ratios adhere more closely to the average.

The general planning standard for park and playground space is given as a ratio of acres to population unit. This ratio is one acre of park-playground area to each 100 persons, although few communities have realized this standard. The land use survey of fifty-three central cities reveals that only five communities have reached this goal, and only two of these—Davenport, Iowa, and Dallas, Tex.—are cities of over 50,000 population. The average in the fifty-three central cities is 0.46 acres per 100 persons. When the data are summarized by population groups, the following averages are obtained.

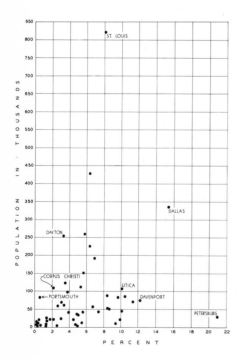

Fig. 21. Parks and Playgrounds. Percentage of total developed area.

NUMBER OF CITIES	POPULATION GROUP	PARKS AND PLAYGROUNDS ACRES PER 100 PERSONS
28	50,000 or less	0.51
13	50,000 – 100,000	0.52
7	100,000 – 250,000	0.46
5	250,000 and over	0.43

It can be seen that while all four population groups average close to 0.50 acres per 100 persons, the central city has only about half the amount of land generally accepted as a minimum standard. However, it is shown in Figure 22 that, although these averages do illustrate the paucity of park area in our cities, they are not adequate descriptions of the individual ratios. It is apparent from this scatter diagram that the ratio of land used for parks and playgrounds to the population is not dependent on city size, and that in each group there are wide variations.

Variations in the proportion of park area in cities reflect local differences in policy. In smaller communities where the countryside is close at hand and there are generous private grounds available, the demand for public parks and playgrounds is appreciably less than in the large, densely developed city. While we have noted the tendency for park land, as a percentage of the developed area, to increase with the population, it is clear that the need is not ade-

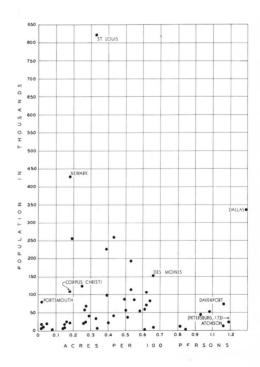

Fig. 22. Parks and Playgrounds. Acres per 100 persons.

quately met in most communities. In the first place, this results from a lack of foresight in acquiring public areas in advance of need. In the second place, once property values have been forced up by urban development most communities are reluctant to compete in the land market on an equal footing with private enterprise. As an unhappy consequence park space is not only inadequate but poorly distributed. In theory, an effort should be made to distribute these public areas over the city in accordance with the population pattern, but in practice political and market considerations often cause spatial inequities, and the major amount of park land is found in one or two holdings.

PUBLIC AND SEMIPUBLIC PROPERTY

Institutions such as churches, clubs, schools, police and fire stations, governmental buildings, and other public or quasi-public establishments classified as public and semipublic property occupy an average of almost 11 per cent of the developed area of the city. These are the averages by population group.

NUMBER OF CITIES	POPULATION GROUP	PUBLIC AND SEMIPUBLIC PROPERTY PERCENTAGE OF TOTAL DEVELOPED AREA
28	50,000 or less	13.25
13	50,000 – 100,000	10.82
7	100,000 – 250,000	11.22
5	250,000 and over	9.59

While these averages seem to indicate a rather constant proportion of public land to the developed areas, actually the ranges in all four population groups are wide (see Figure 23). For example, the range for the fifty-three cities is 2.01 to 53.75 per cent. Centralia, Ill., has the low ratio whereas Williamsburg, Va., has the unusually high ratio. In cities of less than 50,000 population, six cities have over 20 per cent of their developed area in public and semipublic uses: Marshall, Mich. (21.94 per cent), Frankfort, Ky. (24.56 per cent), Mexico, Mo. (25.98 per cent), Santa Fe, N. M. (27.87 per cent), Roswell, N. M. (31.63 per cent), and Williamsburg, Va. (53.75 per cent). All of these have some special feature, an airport, private schools, or state capitol grounds, that make them atypical examples. Excluding these cities, the ranges found in each population group are relatively wide or generally between 4 and 20 per cent of the total developed area. The number and type of facilities

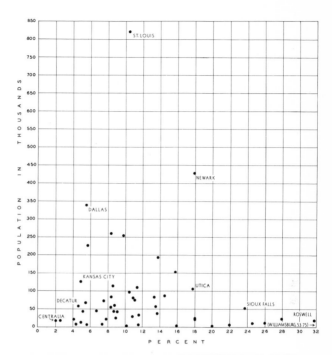

Fig. 23. Public and Semipublic Property. Percentage of total developed area.

vary from community to community according to local needs, affecting the percentage of developed area used for these purposes. Large public uses, institutions, and cemeteries are cases in point. Furthermore, in the case of state or county seats of government an unusually large proportion of the developed area may be given over to public building groups. Other cities have within their boundaries hospitals, institutions, or colleges which may serve a regional or state-wide area.

The average ratio for public and semipublic areas is 0.75 acres per one hundred persons, with a range of 0.15 to 17.35 acres. The average ratios for the four population groups are as follows:

NUMBER OF CITIES	POPULATION GROUP	PUBLIC AND SEMIPUBLIC PROPERTY ACRES PER 100 PERSONS
28	50,000 or less	1.32
13	50,000 – 100,000	0.87
7	100,000 – 250,000	0.90
5	250,000 and over	0.48

There is a tendency for the amount of land for this use to decrease with an increase in population, although, because of the wide variations already noted in individual cities no definite trend or relationship can be assumed (see Figure 24).

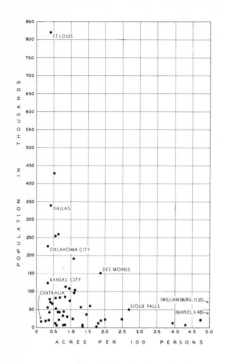

Fig. 24. Public and Semipublic Property. Acres per 100 persons.

SUMMARY OF USES

A surprisingly large proportion of the city is devoted to nonprivate use. When we summarize the area devoted to railroads, streets, parks, playgrounds, and public and semipublic uses, it is found that an average of 50.63 per cent of the total developed area is so used, with the remaining 49.37 per cent used for the private purposes of residences, commerce, and industry.

NUMBER OF CITIES	POPULATION GROUP	PERCENTAGE OF TOTAL DEVELOPED AREA PRIVATELY DEVELOPED	PERCENTAGE OF TOTAL DEVELOPED AREA PUBLICLY DEVELOPED
28	50,000 or less	48.35	51.65
13	50,000 – 100,000	44.53	55.47
7	100,000 – 250,000	50.14	49.86
5	250,000 and over	52.69	47.31

The use of urban land is about equally divided between public and private uses. In two of these groups there is a slight variation in favor of publicly developed property.

As noted in a previous section, the total utilization per unit of population decreases as the population increases. This is true also for the two divisions of privately and publicly developed property.

NUMBER OF CITIES	POPULATION GROUP	ACRES PER 100 PERSONS PRIVATELY DEVELOPED	PUBLICLY DEVELOPED	TOTAL DEVELOPED
28	50,000 or less	4.82	5.15	9.97
13	50,000 – 100,000	3.57	4.44	8.01
7	100,000 – 250,000	4.03	4.00	8.03
5	250,000 and over	2.66	2.38	5.04

The average amount of urban land used is 6.89 acres per 100 persons. Large cities have less than this, as shown by the above averages, and small cities usually have more.

The amount of privately developed area occupied by residential, commercial, and industrial uses remains relatively constant for the four population groups.

NUMBER OF CITIES	POPULATION GROUP	PRIVATELY DEVELOPED AREAS PERCENTAGE OF TOTAL DEVELOPED AREAS RESIDENTIAL	COMMERCIAL	INDUSTRIAL
28	50,000 or less	39.56	3.14	5.65
13	50,000 – 100,000	37.16	2.58	4.79
7	100,000 – 250,000	41.40	2.90	5.84
5	250,000 and over	39.97	4.26	8.46

This again shows the relatively constant relationship that exists between the land absorbed for private use and the total developed area.

In percentage of total developed land used for public and semi-public purposes, there are greater variations between individual cities. These are reflected in the larger differences among the group averages.

NUMBER OF CITIES	POPULATION GROUP	PUBLICLY DEVELOPED AREAS PERCENTAGE OF TOTAL DEVELOPED AREA RAILROADS	STREETS	PARKS AND PLAYGROUNDS	PUBLIC AND SEMI-PUBLIC
28	50,000 or less	4.99	28.33	5.08	13.25
13	50,000 – 100,000	4.85	33.27	6.53	10.82
7	100,000 – 250,000	5.39	27.57	5.68	11.22
5	250,000 and over	4.38	24.75	8.59	9.59

In conclusion, there are significant variations among central cities as to how, and how much, urban land is used. These differences arise from social and economic characteristics of individual cities and are influenced to a considerable degree by regional and national economic factors. Where the demand for land is predicated on local factors, such as housing, we find a high correlation between

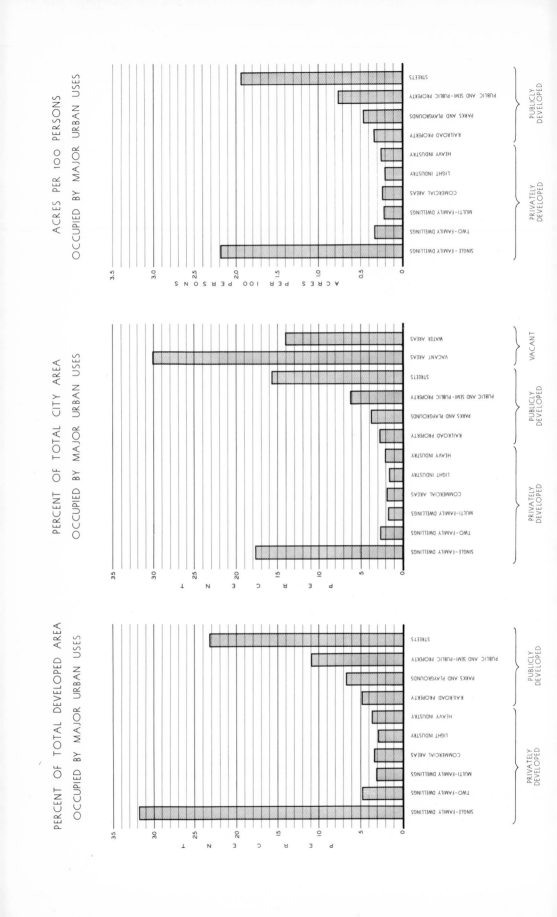

PERCENT OF TOTAL DEVELOPED AREA
OCCUPIED BY MAJOR URBAN USES

PERCENT OF TOTAL CITY AREA
OCCUPIED BY MAJOR URBAN USES

ACRES PER 100 PERSONS
OCCUPIED BY MAJOR URBAN USES

land absorption and population. On the other hand, where the service of land has an economic base extending beyond the city, variations between cities are greater, and there is little relationship between use and population. Heavy industry and railroads are examples of this. The demand for land for public use is not, in a strict sense, stimulated by economic incentives. There is a generally accepted standard which applies to the amount so used, and sites are usually selected for the convenience of the persons to be served. Nevertheless, the amount of land devoted to streets, parks, playgrounds, and other public and semipublic uses is dependent on local policies and politics, and accordingly wide variations are found among cities of about the same size. The amount of land required for urban development for the fifty-three central cities is shown graphically on Plate X.

VACANT AREAS

The average central city, as defined by the political boundary, often contains more land than is necessary for urban development. This vacant land, together with the water areas contained within the city's boundaries, composes the undeveloped acreage of a city, which in some cases is as much as 88.65 per cent of the official corporate area. The preceding analyses have been based solely on the developed areas of the cities. However, the variously developed land areas, figured as a percentage of the total city area, are shown in Table 1. In many cases, these percentages are not meaningful because of the arbitrary character of city boundaries.

In general smaller cities have a higher percentage of vacant land than larger ones. Percentages of vacant land for the various population groups are shown below.

NUMBER OF CITIES	POPULATION GROUP	VACANT AREAS PERCENTAGE OF TOTAL CITY AREA
28	50,000 or less	47.01
13	50,000 – 100,000	38.80
7	100,000 – 250,000	21.85
5	250,000 and over	20.37

As an overall average, about one-third of the total city area of the fifty-three central cities surveyed was vacant or unused for urban purposes. The vacant areas of five typical cities are shown on Plate XI.

UTICA NEW YORK

SCALE

LINCOLN, NEBRASKA

SCALE

VACANT AREAS

LEGEND

PARKS & OPEN SPACES

CENTRAL BUSINESS DI

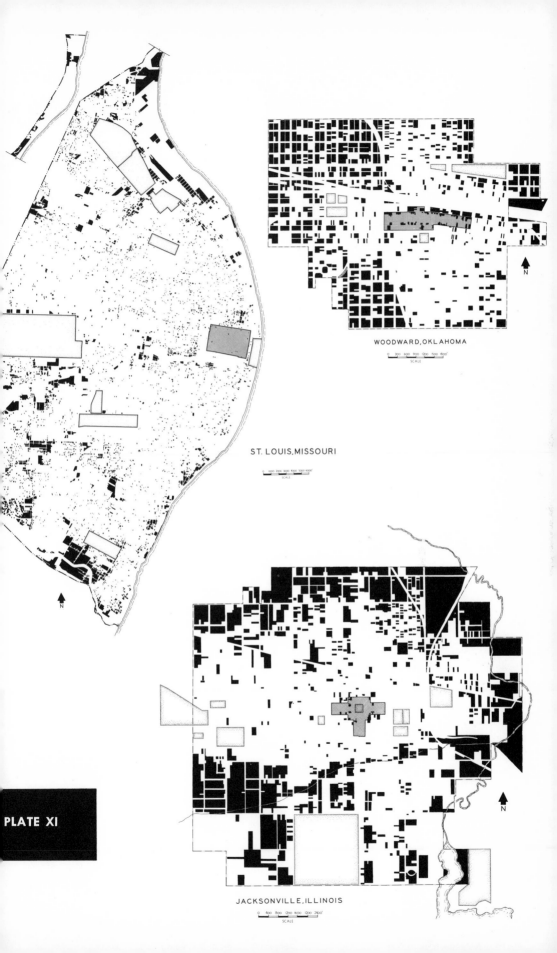

WOODWARD, OKLAHOMA

SCALE

ST. LOUIS, MISSOURI

SCALE

JACKSONVILLE, ILLINOIS

SCALE

PLATE XI

4

THE SATELLITE CITY

Decentralization of urban population and institutions has been an important factor in the development of satellite communities near the periphery of the city—suburban towns more or less independent, yet in many ways clearly subordinate to the large city around which they have clustered. The growth of urban areas has been erratic and without pattern. Instead of an even spread in successive concentric circles, this growth has been sometimes rapid, sometimes slow, along major radial thoroughfares first, and next in the wedges between, but often jumping beyond all existing urban development to form new nucleations (see Plate XII). The political consequence has been the creation of a multiplicity of minor governmental units, each performing one or more functions necessary in the urban complex.

There are two major types of suburbs in American urban areas, the suburb of production and the suburb of consumption. As commercial and industrial organizations are crowded out of central cities because of their inability to compete with other economic enterprises for space, they tend to settle in suburban areas and attract workers to them. In time, residential colonies of workers develop near the industries in which they work, as in the case of East Chicago, Ind., or East St. Louis, Ill. These suburbs are primarily areas of production and are often less dependent upon the central city than are satellites that exist only as "dormitory" towns.

The suburb of consumption is in direct contrast with the indus-

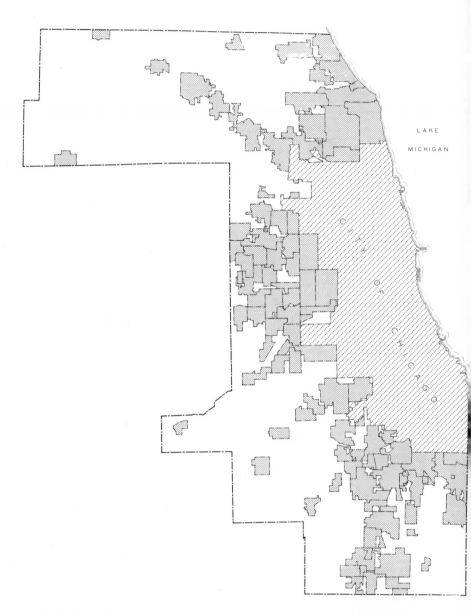

PLATE XII. Cook County, Illinois. The fringes of large central cities are being divided into a multiplicity of small disjointed incorporations.

trial satellite. Both types are in a sense residential suburbs, but whereas the resident of the industrialized suburb finds employment in his own community, the inhabitants of the dormitory suburb are generally employed in the central city. Seldom, however, does the individual suburb fall strictly within one or the other of these classifications. There are numerous varieties, each suburban area being shaped and colored by local economic activities, traditions, and social outlook.

The thirty-three cities included in this land use analysis range between 900 and 74,347 in population. These cities have been grouped into four population size groups: less than 5,000; 5,000 to 10,000; 10,000 to 25,000; and 25,000 and over. Data from the thirty-three land use surveys forming the basis of this study are tabulated in Tables 5 and 6. These tabulations are of the same form used for central cities. In Table 5 the area devoted to the major uses of urban land is expressed as a percentage of the total developed area of the city, and then as a percentage of the total city area. In Table 6 the amount of land used is expressed as a ratio of area to population, or acres per 100 persons. In addition, summaries by population groups are contained in Tables 7 and 8.

DEVELOPED AREAS

Of the total area found within the boundaries of the thirty-three satellite municipalities, 63.88 per cent is developed for some urban use. Of the 36.12 per cent undeveloped, 35.45 per cent is vacant land, while 0.67 per cent consists of water areas. Comparisons between these figures and the same percentages for central cities are not meaningful, because both are based on total city area, and therefore dependent on arbitrary boundaries and geographical features. The central cities, for example, contain an average of 14.05 per cent of their total areas in water areas.

The percentage for developed area varies in the different population groups as follows.

NUMBER OF CITIES	POPULATION GROUP	TOTAL DEVELOPED AREA PERCENTAGE OF TOTAL CITY AREA
7	5,000 or less	36.15
6	5,000 – 10,000	57.22
10	10,000 – 25,000	62.23
10	25,000 and over	77.12

There is an evident tendency for large satellite communities to develop a higher percentage of their total area than small ones. However, examination of the individual cities shows large deviations from the pattern and suggests that population is not the major factor in percentage of area developed.

The more recent growth of the metropolis has been centrifugal in nature, and seldom confined to a particular segment of the peripheral area. Rather than attaching itself to an existing community, much of this development has "leapfrogged" older satellites to create new communities, each incorporating a generous amount of land for future development. An example of the effect of this type of growth on local government boundaries is found in the Chicago urbanized area (see Plate XII). According to the 1950 United States Census, there were 118 cities, towns, and villages within this urbanized area. Whatever these forces of growth tend to produce in the way of land absorption, with the empirical methods used to define the city area, no relationship can be expected between the developed area and the total corporate area.

When the ratios of developed area to population are compared for the thirty-three suburban cities, we find a positive relationship.

NUMBER OF CITIES	POPULATION GROUP	TOTAL DEVELOPED AREA ACRES PER 100 PERSONS
7	5,000 or less	27.00
6	5,000 – 10,000	21.43
10	10,000 – 25,000	13.24
10	25,000 and over	5.77

The larger suburban cities have fewer acres of urban development per 100 persons than have the smaller cities. This is the same relationship found in the central cities, for the larger the city, the smaller the area of development per unit of population. The range in ratios in the smaller cities, those with populations of less than 5,000, are extremely wide—between 13.17 and 58.92 acres per 100 persons.* In the next group, there is a range between 11.73 and 38.52 acres per unit of population. In cities of between 10,000 to 25,000 population the range is 7.14 to 25.15 acres per 100 persons. The range among the larger cities is more narrow—only 2.95 to 9.83 acres of developed land per 100 persons.

---

* Wide variations may be expected in this group. Since the populations of these cities are small, relatively small acreages produce wide variations in percentages.

RESIDENTIAL AREAS

In suburban cities, the largest demand on use of land is residential. This use in the satellite community absorbs 41.98 per cent of the developed area. The proportion of the total developed area utilized by housing ranges between 9.13 per cent and 68.95 per cent; however, the majority of cities surveyed are within a range between 30 and 60 per cent. Cities with the lowest proportions are Morton Grove, Ill. (9.13), Skokie, Ill. (11.08), Lincolnwood, Ill. (11.85), and East Chicago, Ind. (12.56). In contrast to the low percentages found in these suburbs, the dormitory communities of Glendale, Ohio, Richmond Heights, Mo., and Falls Church, Va., have 68.95, 68.31, and 67.12 per cent, respectively, of their total area devoted to dwelling use. A wide variation is found between the percentages for individual suburbs and averages for each of the population groups.

NUMBER OF CITIES	POPULATION GROUP	RESIDENTIAL AREA PERCENTAGE OF TOTAL DEVELOPED AREA
7	5,000 or less	27.47
6	5,000 – 10,000	37.52
10	10,000 – 25,000	51.17
10	25,000 and over	40.24

The larger cities have a greater proportion of their developed area in residential use than do the smaller cities. This is perhaps a reflection of the intensity of use in the older and larger satellites. It will be noted that cities of over 25,000 population have devoted only 40.24 per cent of their developed area to residential use—or less than the 41.98 per cent average for all thirty-three satellite cities. The cities in this population group have relatively high housing densities, but more important, they include heavily industrialized suburbs such as East Chicago and East St. Louis.

The areas used for residential purposes, when expressed in terms of acres per 100 persons, show a relationship according to the size of population.

NUMBER OF CITIES	POPULATION GROUP	RESIDENTIAL AREA ACRES PER 100 PERSONS
7	5,000 or less	7.42
6	5,000 – 10,000	8.04
10	10,000 – 25,000	6.77
10	25,000 and over	2.33

The larger cities on an average have fewer acres of dwelling area per unit of population than have the smaller cities. Of the thirty-three cities, East Chicago, Ind., and Glendale, Ohio, have extreme ratios of 1.10 acres and 18.13 acres. The widest range of ratios are found in the two groups of less than 10,000 population—14.57 among the smallest cities and 8.74 among the second group. There is a range of 5.63 acres per 100 persons in suburbs with population of 10,000 to 25,000, but only a 4.64-acre range in cities with populations of over 25,000. Although we find some wide variations from the group averages in the cities studied, there seems to be a relationship between the ratio of residential land to population and the size of the satellite city. The smallest suburbs have the largest residential areas for their number of residents. The lower density of development found in suburban areas, as contrasted with the central city, is evident from a comparison of figures. Where 3.65 acres per 100 persons is used for dwelling purposes in suburban communities, only 2.73 acres were required to accommodate the same number of persons in the central city.

Before turning to the major subdivisions of residential use, it is important to note something of the local nature of the housing market. We have mentioned that the demand for a particular type of housing structure is conditioned by factors peculiar to the community. Personal preferences, economic forces, and social customs produce a demand pattern unique in a given city. In the suburban community such local individuality is often more pronounced than that of the central city. This is due in the first instance to the fact that the suburb is often the product of one or a group of enterprises. Land is bought, subdivided, and marketed as a site for a particular type of housing structure. Thus either by the personal preference of the real estate developer or by the collective desires of the inhabitants, expressed through their choice of purchase, a satellite community may become an exclusively single-family suburb or one of mixed residential uses with one type predominating. After initial development, the inhabitants of a suburb may restrict the use of land to selected activities and housing structures through zoning and land covenants. Another type of individualized suburb is the "mill village" where an industry has a proprietary control over housing and a multifamily suburb is most likely to be developed.

SINGLE-FAMILY DWELLING AREAS

The single-family dwelling area occupies a greater percentage of the developed area of the satellite city than any other public or private use. An average of 36.18 per cent of the total developed area of the city is devoted to this use. Among the smaller cities the land utilized by this subdivision of the dwelling area ranges from 8.33 per cent to 65.52 per cent with an average of 26.41 per cent. In the next larger group of cities, those of 5,000 to 10,000 population, the range is 9.43 per cent to 64.93 per cent of the total developed area. The average for this group is 35.55 per cent. All of the cities with populations between 10,000 and 25,000 are within a spread of about 26 per cent, and all, interestingly, are higher than the average of 36.18 per cent found for all thirty-three cities. The average utilization is 47.83 per cent of the total developed area. Since the larger cities surveyed vary from the industrial suburb to the typical dormitory community in character, it is not surprising that there is a wide range in the single-family use, between 7.14 per cent and 53.32 per cent—East Chicago, Ind., possessing the lower proportion and Beverly Hills, Calif., the higher. The average found for this group, however, is 30.98 per cent of the developed area. The average for each of the population groups is as follows.

NUMBER OF CITIES	POPULATION GROUP	SINGLE-FAMILY DWELLING PERCENTAGE OF TOTAL DEVELOPED AREA
7	5,000 or less	26.41
6	5,000 – 10,000	35.55
10	10,000 – 25,000	47.83
10	25,000 and over	30.98

The average number of acres per 100 persons used in suburban communities for single-family dwellings is 3.14. For these thirty-three cities, the minimum number of acres utilized per 100 persons is 0.62 (East Chicago, Ind.) and the maximum is 17.46 (Northfield, Ill.). The widest range in ratios occurs in the cities of less than 5,000 population. In this group Morton Grove, Ill., has 3.30 acres per 100 persons while Northfield, Ill., has 17.46 acres per 100 persons. In the group of cities in the 5,000 to 10,000 population bracket there is a range of about 9 acres between Skokie, Ill. (2.69), and West Vancouver, B. C. (11.66). The range for cities of 10,000 to 25,000 population is between 3.32 acres and 9.32 acres per person while in cities of over 25,000, there is a range of 0.62 to 5.06 acres per population unit. The strikingly low ratio of 0.62 acres per 100 persons belongs, as noted above, to East Chicago.

Despite the wide differences in the two variables, there is an apparent relationship between the acreage ratios for single-family dwelling areas and the population groups. Where the cities are arranged in order of magnitude, it is seen that the largest cities have the smallest ratios. The very low group average for cities of 25,000 and over is due to the inclusion of highly industrialized cities, together with the higher density characteristic of larger cities.

NUMBER OF CITIES	POPULATION GROUP	SINGLE-FAMILY DWELLINGS ACRES PER 100 PERSONS
7	5,000 or less	7.13
6	5,000 – 10,000	7.62
10	10,000 – 25,000	6.33
10	25,000 and over	1.79

The popularity of the single-family dwelling structure in suburban areas is strikingly illustrated by the fact that 3.14 acres per 100 persons is devoted to this use, whereas only 2.19 acres per unit of population are utilized for single-family dwellings in the central city.

TWO-FAMILY DWELLING AREAS

The two-family dwelling ranks second in popularity as a housing structure in suburban areas. In contrast with the large area utilized by single-family dwellings, two-family dwellings occupy a small area. Moreover, the two-family dwelling is of relatively less importance as a type of housing structure in suburban areas than in the central city. In the satellite cities, only 7.88 per cent of the total dwelling area is occupied by two-family structures; the comparable average for central cities is 12.11 per cent.

In the thirty-three satellite cities, an average of 3.31 per cent of the total developed area is utilized for two-family dwelling purposes. One of the most striking features found in comparing areas in two-family use is the wide variation among different cities. The range is between 0.00 per cent and 14.47 per cent of the developed area. The larger suburban cities have a greater proportion of their developed area in two-family use; satellites of the larger cities, moreover, rank highest in this usage. Irvington, East Orange, and

Bloomfield, cities in the New York-New Jersey urbanized area, devote 14.47, 11.60, and 6.42 per cent of their respective areas to two-family dwellings. Similarly, Oak Park and Maywood, of the Chicago conurbation, and Richmond Heights and East St. Louis, of the St. Louis metropolitan area, have relatively high averages. However, these cities are exceptional, for two-thirds of the satellite cities have less than the average proportion of 3.31 per cent found for all satellite communities, and nearly one-half of the cities have less than 1.00 per cent of their developed areas in two-family use. When the area devoted to this use is summarized by population groups, it is seen that the percentage of total developed area used tends to increase as the population increases and that in the suburban community, as in the central city, this type of structure tends to predominate in the larger and eastern communities.

NUMBER OF CITIES	POPULATION GROUP	TWO-FAMILY DWELLINGS PERCENTAGE OF TOTAL DEVELOPED AREA
7	5,000 or less	0.91
6	5,000 – 10,000	1.06
10	10,000 – 25,000	1.79
10	25,000 and over	5.33

The range in such use expressed as acres per 100 persons is also wide. Two cities, Winnetka, Ill., and Berkeley, Mo., have ratios of 0.00 acres, while Glendale, Ohio, a suburb of Cincinnati, has the opposite extreme of 0.74 acres per 100 persons. The group with less than 5,000 population contains both extremes. The differences in ratios of cities in other population groups are not as great. New Westminster, B. C., is the only community with a population exceeding 25,000 persons having a ratio of less than 0.23 acres per 100 persons.

NUMBER OF CITIES	POPULATION GROUP	TWO-FAMILY DWELLINGS ACRES PER 100 PERSONS
7	5,000 or less	0.25
6	5,000 – 10,000	0.23
10	10,000 – 25,000	0.24
10	25,000 and over	0.31

From this table it can be seen that regardless of city size, the proportionate area devoted to two-family dwellings remains relatively stable. This is also true of central cities, although central cities on an average devote about 0.04 acres more land to two-family use per 100 persons than suburban communities.

MULTIFAMILY DWELLING AREAS

The larger suburban cities have a higher average percentage of their developed areas occupied by multifamily residences than do central cities. The increase in the number of apartments constructed with the aid of FHA-insured loans, linked with the centrifugal move to the suburbs, largely accounts for this high percentage. Almost 4 per cent of the developed area of the ten satellite cities with populations over 25,000 is in multifamily use compared with an average of 3.01 per cent for fifty-three central cities.

NUMBER OF CITIES	POPULATION GROUP	MULTIFAMILY DWELLINGS PERCENTAGE OF TOTAL DEVELOPED AREA
7	5,000 or less	0.15
6	5,000 – 10,000	0.91
10	10,000 – 25,000	1.55
10	25,000 and over	3.93

Smaller suburban cities have a small percentage of their developed area in multifamily dwelling use. Three cities of less than 5,000 population have no multifamily dwellings whatever; three of the other four cities in the group have less than 0.10 per cent of their developed area so occupied. In the group of cities with populations between 5,000 and 10,000, only two of the six cities devote over 1.00 per cent of the developed area to this use. Three satellites of St. Louis, Mo.—Brentwood, Clayton, and Richmond Heights— have the highest proportions in the next group. Brentwood, with 12.06 per cent of the developed area in multifamily use, vies with East Orange, N. J. (of the largest city-size group), for the highest proportion of multifamily dwelling area. East Orange, frequently called an "apartment city," has 12.19 per cent of its developed area occupied by multifamily dwelling structures. All the cities of 25,000 and over have more than 3 per cent of their developed area so utilized except East St. Louis, Ill., East Chicago, Ind., and the Canadian city of West Vancouver.

The multifamily dwelling area forms only 5.93 per cent of the total dwelling area compared to 7.60 per cent for the central cities. On an average this subdivision of the dwelling area uses only 0.22 acres of land to accommodate 100 persons, or virtually the same ratio found in the central cities.

Although there are wide differences among the individual cities surveyed, the tendency is for the area per population to increase as the city size increases. This tendency is evident when the cities are arranged according to population.

NUMBER OF CITIES	POPULATION GROUP	MULTIFAMILY DWELLINGS ACRES PER 100 PERSONS
7	5,000 or less	0.04
6	5,000 – 10,000	0.19
10	10,000 – 25,000	0.20
10	25,000 and over	0.23

Only one city in the lower population group has over 0.05 of an acre of multifamily use per 100 persons, and three cities, as mentioned above, do not have any multifamily development within their corporate limits. Three cities in the 5,000 to 10,000 population group have ratios of less than 0.05 acres, although one city, Falls Church, Va., has a ratio of 0.62 acres per 100 persons. The range in ratios for cities of 10,000 to 25,000 is from 0.03 acres to 0.87 acres per 100 persons. In the larger cities, those having populations of over 25,000, the range is between 0.04 acres and 0.44 acres per 100 persons.

SUMMARY OF RESIDENTIAL USES

In suburban cities residential uses account for almost half of the total developed area, about 42 per cent, in fact. This average is slightly higher than the percentage of total developed area utilized for all residential purposes in the central city. The importance of the residential area in the urban pattern is clearly evident from the following table.

	THIRTY-THREE CITIES	
TYPE OF USE	PERCENTAGE OF TOTAL DEVELOPED AREA	PERCENTAGE OF TOTAL RESIDENTIAL AREA
Single-family dwellings	36.18	86.19
Two-family dwellings	3.31	7.88
Multifamily dwellings	2.49	5.93
Total residential	41.98	100.00

The single-family dwelling in the thirty-three suburban cities occupy 86.19 per cent of the residential area, while in the central cities it occupies 80.29 per cent.

The popularity of the single-family dwelling in satellite communities results in less area being devoted to double and multifamily structures. Only 3.31 per cent of the developed area of the satellites is occupied by two-family dwellings as compared with the 4.79 per cent so occupied in central cities. The multifamily dwelling area in satellite cities forms 2.49 per cent of the total developed area, while 3.01 per cent of the developed area of central cities is thus used.

The residential area covers 80.15 per cent, or almost four-fifths, of all privately developed land in the suburban community.

We now deal with the land used for commercial, industrial, recreational, and public and semipublic service activities. Almost three-fifths of the developed areas of satellite cities are given over to these uses that provide the economic lifeblood of the community and the necessary services and amenities for urban living.

COMMERCIAL AREAS

Commercial areas in satellite cities, on an average, occupy 2.54 per cent of the total developed area, somewhat less than the 3.32 per cent utilized for commerce in the central cities. As might be expected, the range in proportions of land so used is greater in satellite communities than in central cities. The proportion of the total developed area ranges between 0.51 per cent and 6.39 per cent. The number of inhabitants in a community is a factor in the demand for certain types of commercial outlets and services. For example, we do not expect to find large department stores in small communities. More important in the case of suburban cities is their proximity to larger and more diversified shopping centers. If these centers are within convenient travel distance, the demand for local outlets is markedly reduced, the greater demand being for shops and services filling day-to-day wants. However, as the conurbation spreads and the central city becomes more remote, the need for a more diversified center becomes greater. Eventually, the comparatively wide separation of the central business district from the homes of a large number of people results in the formation of sub-centers rivaling the downtown district in scope and diversity of establishments. This has been the case, for instance, in Clayton, Mo., where St. Louis's three largest department stores have established large suburban stores, as has happened in numerous other

American cities. These factors have been instrumental in increasing the proportion of commercial use in the larger suburban cities to approximately that of central cities, especially in the satellites of the larger metropolises. As a result, there is a general tendency for this land use to increase directly with an increase in population.

Yet the variations found between individual suburban cities within each population group would seem to indicate that certain factors—such as travel distances to major commercial centers, social status, and family income or purchasing power—are more important in creating a demand for this service of land than the particular number of inhabitants. The range in cities of less than 5,000 persons is between 0.60 and 5.34 per cent, while in cities of 5,000 to 10,000 it is between 0.51 and 3.23 per cent of the developed area. In the next two groups, cities with populations between 10,000 and 25,000 have a range between 1.05 and 3.32 per cent, and cities of over 25,000 population between 1.28 and 6.39 per cent. The averages for the various groups follow.

NUMBER OF CITIES	POPULATION GROUP	COMMERCIAL AREAS PERCENTAGE OF TOTAL DEVELOPED AREA
7	5,000 or less	3.03
6	5,000 – 10,000	1.43
10	10,000 – 25,000	2.09
10	25,000 and over	3.10

When ratios of the amount of land used to the population unit are compared, a trend is observed. The smaller cities have a larger commercial area per unit of population than do the larger cities.

NUMBER OF CITIES	POPULATION GROUP	COMMERCIAL AREAS ACRES PER 100 PERSONS
7	5,000 or less	0.82
6	5,000 – 10,000	0.31
10	10,000 – 25,000	0.28
10	25,000 and over	0.18

The range for the smaller cities is between 0.15 acres and 2.12 acres per 100 persons. In the second group the range is much narrower, between 0.14 acres and 0.47 acres per 100 persons. The ten cities ranging in population between 10,000 and 25,000 persons have between 0.10 acres and 0.61 acres per 100 persons. The range for the larger cities is between 0.11 acres and 0.52 acres per 100 persons, although the upper extreme represents a wide deviation from the norm of this group. If Beverly Hills, Calif., is removed from this group, the range then becomes 0.11 to 0.25 acres per 100 persons.

LIGHT AND HEAVY INDUSTRY

The data for light and heavy industry have been combined for all satellite cities, since in several cases these classifications were combined in the original survey, and separate data are not available.

The percentage of developed land occupied by industry is significantly greater than the proportion found in central cities. The average for thirty-three suburban cities is 7.86 per cent, for the fifty-three central cities 6.44 per cent, of the total developed area.

NUMBER OF CITIES	POPULATION GROUP	LIGHT AND HEAVY INDUSTRY PERCENTAGE OF TOTAL DEVELOPED AREA
7	5,000 or less	6.55
6	5,000 – 10,000	2.49
10	10,000 – 25,000	1.60
10	25,000 and over	13.57

In the first group Bettendorf, Iowa, is high with a percentage of 29.47. The range, excluding Bettendorf, is between 0.25 per cent and 6.35 per cent of the developed area. The range in the second group—cities of between 5,000 and 10,000 population—is between 0.19 per cent and 5.46 per cent. In cities of 10,000 to 25,000 persons the range is from 0.03 per cent (University Park, Tex.) to 12.84 per cent (Brentwood, Mo.) of the developed area; however, all but two cities lie within a range of 0.03 to 1.46 per cent. The prevalence of heavy industry in the larger cities, together with a generally higher incidence of light industry, gives these cities a range of from 1.02 per cent in Beverly Hills, Calif., to 54.08 per cent in East Chicago, Ind. All cities except East Chicago, however, have percentages of 10.64 or less.

It is apparent from these ranges that there is little correlation between the area used for all industrial purposes in satellite cities and the total developed area. There is a corresponding lack of any constant relationship between area and a given unit of population.

NUMBER OF CITIES	POPULATION GROUP	LIGHT AND HEAVY INDUSTRY ACRES PER 100 PERSONS
7	5,000 or less	1.77
6	5,000 – 10,000	0.53
10	10,000 – 25,000	0.21
10	25,000 and over	0.78

The ranges for these groups are: 0.07 to 4.62, 0.07 to 1.41, 0.00 to 0.93, and 0.06 to 4.75 acres per 100 persons. These variations are due both to the position of the community in the economic milieu and to self-imposed restrictions of industrial development. Industry is eschewed in many suburban centers; in others, a normal complement of service industries is found, but manufacturing industries are partly or wholly excluded. At the other extreme, we find satellite centers that developed in the first instance as industrial areas, with housing a subsequent development.

RAILROAD PROPERTY

All but one of the thirty-three suburban cities surveyed have some railroad property within their corporate limits. Bloomfield, N. J., is the one exception. The average percentage of developed area in suburban cities used for railroad purposes is 4.65, approximately that found for central cities.

		RAILROAD PROPERTY	
NUMBER OF CITIES	POPULATION GROUP	PERCENTAGE OF TOTAL DEVELOPED AREA	ACRES PER 100 PERSONS
7	5,000 or less	4.53	1.22
6	5,000 – 10,000	3.83	0.82
10	10,000 – 25,000	3.03	0.40
10	25,000 and over	5.91	0.34

The amount of land devoted to railroad usage varies considerably between cities. The range for the thirty-three cities (excluding Bloomfield, N. J.) is between 0.18 per cent and 13.94 per cent of the total developed area. The ratios of land to population range between 0.02 acres and 5.30 acres per 100 persons for the thirty-three cities.

COMBINED LIGHT AND HEAVY INDUSTRY AND RAILROADS

When all industrial uses and railroad property are combined, the following averages are found.

		COMBINED INDUSTRY AND RAILROAD PROPERTY	
NUMBER OF CITIES	POPULATION GROUP	PERCENTAGE OF TOTAL DEVELOPED AREA	ACRES PER 100 PERSONS
7	5,000 or less	11.08	2.99
6	5,000 – 10,000	6.32	1.35
10	10,000 – 25,000	4.63	0.61
10	25,000 and over	19.48	1.12

The variations within each population group are considerable, and no consistent relationships between the area used and total developed area, or between the area used and population, are apparent.

STREETS

Streets occupy the second greatest amount of land in suburban cities. An average of 27.67 per cent of the developed area is devoted to streets, alleys, highways, and other public and private thoroughfares. As previously shown, an average of 28.10 per cent of the developed area of the central city was so used. The following summary shows the findings for all satellite cities.

NUMBER OF CITIES	POPULATION GROUP	STREETS PERCENTAGE OF TOTAL DEVELOPED AREA
7	5,000 or less	32.56
6	5,000 – 10,000	33.17
10	10,000 – 25,000	24.71
10	25,000 and over	26.84

The ranges for these groups are 15.31 to 49.53, 15.27 to 52.59, 17.44 to 36.68, and 13.98 to 37.60 per cent of the developed areas. Twenty-four of the thirty-three cities have between 19 and 35 per cent of their total developed area in streets.

Expressed in terms of population, suburban street areas follow the same pattern observed for central cities, that is, the smaller the city and the lower the density, the greater the proportion of street area.

NUMBER OF CITIES	POPULATION GROUP	STREETS ACRES PER 100 PERSONS
7	5,000 or less	8.79
6	5,000 – 10,000	7.11
10	10,000 – 25,000	3.27
10	25,000 and over	1.55

In this case, however, the difference in ratios between the groups of smallest and largest cities is greater than that found in central cities. The existence of a large number of streets in the speculative subdivisions of smaller and newer suburbs contributes to this disparity.

PARKS AND PLAYGROUNDS

Parks and playgrounds absorb an average of 4.37 per cent of the developed area of satellite cities. Four of the thirty-three cities do not provide public parks and playgrounds. The range for the remaining twenty-nine cities is between 0.05 per cent and 22.23 per cent of the total developed area.

NUMBER OF CITIES	POPULATION GROUP	PARKS AND PLAYGROUNDS PERCENTAGE OF TOTAL DEVELOPED AREA
7	5,000 or less	3.00
6	5,000 – 10,000	7.05
10	10,000 – 25,000	4.65
10	25,000 and over	3.51

This summary shows a reversal of the relationship found in central cities. Instead of the larger cities having the largest proportion of their developed area in parks, the smaller cities show a higher average.

The central cities were rather consistent in providing one-half acre of park for each 100 persons. The following summary for satellite communities shows a marked contrast.

NUMBER OF CITIES	POPULATION GROUP	PARKS AND PLAYGROUNDS ACRES PER 100 PERSONS
7	5,000 or less	0.81
6	5,000 – 10,000	1.51
10	10,000 – 25,000	0.62
10	25,000 and over	0.20

All ten of the largest cities have a deficiency of park and playground area when measured against the general planning standard of one acre per 100 persons. Only two of the cities with a population between 10,000 and 25,000 meet this standard, while two of the thirteen cities of less than 10,000 persons have park areas in excess of one acre per 100 persons. Thus, only four suburban cities meet the standard for park and playground area.

PUBLIC AND SEMIPUBLIC PROPERTY

Public and semipublic uses of land in suburban cities account for an average of 10.93 per cent of the total developed area. The range within each group, however, is wide, and the deviations from the average are many. In general, the larger the city the smaller is the percentage of land devoted to public and semipublic uses.

NUMBER OF CITIES	POPULATION GROUP	PUBLIC AND SEMIPUBLIC PROPERTY PERCENTAGE OF TOTAL DEVELOPED AREA
7	5,000 or less	22.86
6	5,000 – 10,000	14.51
10	10,000 – 25,000	12.75
10	25,000 and over	6.83

Wide deviations are also noted when the utilized area is expressed as a ratio to population. This analysis shows the tendency for small suburban cities to devote a larger area per unit of population to public and semipublic uses than large suburban cities do.

NUMBER OF CITIES	POPULATION GROUP	PUBLIC AND SEMIPUBLIC PROPERTY ACRES PER 100 PERSONS
7	5,000 and less	6.17
6	5,000 – 10,000	3.11
10	10,000 – 25,000	1.69
10	25,000 and over	0.40

SUMMARY OF USES

The amount of land devoted to each urban function in suburban communities is shown graphically on Plate XIII. A large proportion of the developed land is devoted to nonprivate use. When the area devoted to railroads, streets, parks, playgrounds, and other public and semipublic uses is summarized, it is found that an average of 47.62 per cent of the total developed area is so used. The remaining 52.38 per cent is devoted to private development, that is, to residential, commercial, and industrial uses. The proportion of the developed area of satellite cities in public as opposed to private use changes in relation to the population. The smaller cities tend to have a greater percentage of land in public development, and correspondingly less in private use, a relationship shown in the following averages.

NUMBER OF CITIES	POPULATION GROUP	PERCENTAGE OF TOTAL DEVELOPED AREA	
		PRIVATELY DEVELOPED	PUBLICLY DEVELOPED
7	5,000 or less	37.05	62.95
6	5,000 – 10,000	41.44	58.56
10	10,000 – 25,000	54.86	45.14
10	25,000 and over	56.91	43.09

The amount of land developed for each of these two divisions as well as for total urban use per unit of population decreases as the population increases.

NUMBER OF CITIES	POPULATION GROUP	ACRES PER 100 PERSONS		
		PRIVATELY DEVELOPED	PUBLICLY DEVELOPED	TOTAL DEVELOPED
7	5,000 or less	10.01	16.99	27.00
6	5,000 – 10,000	8.88	12.55	21.43
10	10,000 – 25,000	7.26	5.98	13.24
10	25,000 and over	3.28	2.49	5.77

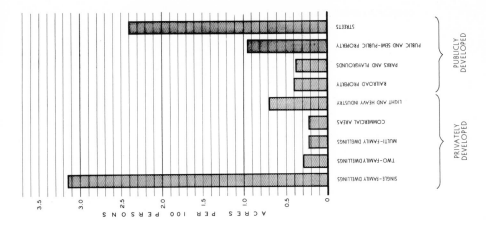

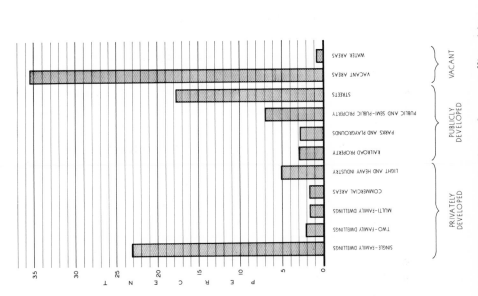

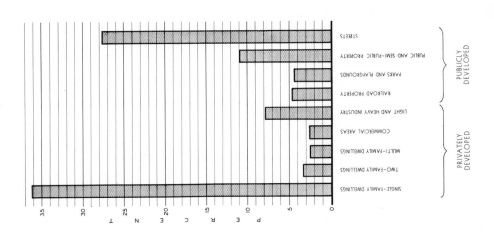

PLATE XIII. Land use in thirty-three satellite cities

The average amount of land used in the thirty-three satellite cities for all urban purposes is 8.69 acres per 100 persons. This is on an average 1.80 acres per 100 persons more than is used for urban purposes in central cities. The ratios of land to population show considerably more variation according to city size than is apparent in the central cities. It will be noted from the summary above that cities of over 25,000 population use for all purposes only about a fifth of the amount of land used by cities with 5,000 or less population.

The percentage of privately developed area occupied by residential, commercial, and industrial uses varies from group to group.

		PRIVATELY DEVELOPED AREAS		
NUMBER OF CITIES	POPULATION GROUP	PERCENTAGE OF TOTAL DEVELOPED AREA		
		RESIDENTIAL	COMMERCIAL	INDUSTRIAL
7	5,000 or less	27.47	3.03	6.55
6	5,000 – 10,000	37.52	1.43	2.49
10	10,000 – 25,000	51.17	2.09	1.60
10	25,000 and over	40.24	3.10	13.57

While there seems to be a general relationship between the percentage of dwelling area and the population, the correlation is not as strong as that observed in central cities. The variations found in the percentage of land used for commercial and industrial purposes in cities of different sizes indicate that little or no relationship can be expected between this percentage and the city's population.

The percentage of the general subdivisions of publicly developed area in suburban cities is shown in the following summary.

		PUBLICLY DEVELOPED AREAS			
		PERCENTAGE OF TOTAL DEVELOPED AREA			
NUMBER OF CITIES	POPULATION GROUP	RAILROADS	STREETS	PARKS AND PLAYGROUNDS	PUBLIC AND SEMIPUBLIC
7	5,000 or less	4.53	32.56	3.00	22.86
6	5,000 – 10,000	3.83	33.17	7.05	14.51
10	10,000 – 25,000	3.03	24.71	4.65	12.75
10	25,000 and over	5.91	26.84	3.51	6.83

In the first three of these subdivisions variations in average according to city size are small and for the most part irregular. In contrast, the averages for public and semipublic uses show a definite relation to population: small suburban cities have, on the average, more of their developed land devoted to these uses than large cities.

In conclusion, the proportion of land in satellite cities that is devoted to urban uses varies considerably among cities. With few exceptions, all major types of urban land uses are represented within each city surveyed, but the quantity of each type varies with the character of the community. There are several factors that govern the quantity of urban space required. To be sure, the same social and economic factors that help shape the central city are present in some degree in the satellite city. But the relatively small size of suburban cities allows the individual more of a share in shaping his environment. Because of these factors there are many kinds of suburbs—each colored by its own economic activities, its traditions, the sentiments and mores of its citizens. There are suburbs industrial in character with little housing and few amenities; there are suburbs representing wealth and social position with remarkably low densities and little commerce or industry; there are also balanced suburbs of homes, business, and industry. Indeed, there is a greater divergency and variety in these satellite towns than there is in the parent city itself; and as each grows and expands it develops an individuality of its own, influenced by the people, businesses, and institutions that move into it.

VACANT AREAS

In addition to the developed land areas previously discussed, the total land areas of cities contain vacant land and water areas. This chapter has so far discussed various land uses as percentages of total developed areas. These land areas are shown in relation to total city areas in Table 5.

As a general rule, a higher percentage of vacant land is found in small cities than in large cities. This was also found to be true in the central cities. Percentages of vacant land for the various population groups are shown below.

NUMBER OF CITIES	POPULATION GROUP	VACANT AREAS PERCENTAGE OF TOTAL CITY AREA
7	5,000 or less	60.51
6	5,000 – 10,000	42.78
10	10,000 – 25,000	37.77
10	25,000 and over	22.28

The average for the thirty-three cities is 35.45 per cent, or slightly more than one-third of the total city area.

5

URBAN AREAS

It will be remembered that space for new population and activities in the city is obtained either by internal rearrangements or shifts of land uses, or by lateral expansion. The easiest place for a city to provide new housing is on the outskirts of its built-up area, where ample land is available at reasonable cost, thus permitting lower population densities and presumably better living conditions. In recent years, we have seen a spectacular centrifugal movement from the central cities to these areas, first of residences, then of institutions, and in some cases the whole complement of economic activities. In almost all cases this development is peripheral and is only an extension of the older city.

The machinery necessary to incorporate this new territory into the city is often complicated and cumbersome. Moreover, the city that spawned this growth is usually helpless, reluctant, or indifferent about annexing this new urbanized territory. In any case the smaller municipalities that have sprung up in the interim are prepared to fight a desperate rear-guard action against becoming an official or political part of the central city. This centrifugal movement has been haphazard and poorly regulated, causing an economic drain on the central city and often a present or future burden on the small political subdivision that suddenly finds it must provide service facilities that may be beyond its means.

In urban areas now there is a growing understanding of what must be accomplished, not only in enlarging the conception of what local government must do (and this includes the planning function), but also in enlarging the area over which local government has jurisdiction. To some this means political annexation by the parent city; to others, some form of "metropolitan" government. To be sure, both of these are aimed at the root of the matter —a recognition that the whole urban area is the "community" and that planning administration and local government, to be effective, must deal comprehensively with the whole, as well as piecemeal with its parts.

The land surveys discussed in the preceding chapters were all confined to the corporate area of the particular city studied. In some cases, the corporate area included the entire built-up area, but for the most part, it contained only a portion of the developed land within the metropolitan community. So that something may be seen of the total complex, we turn to analysis of the whole urban area.

This analysis is based on land use surveys recently completed for eleven urban areas, ranging in size between 7,150 and 119,825 persons. The population of these areas as compared with their central cities is as follows.

	URBAN AREA	CENTRAL CITY
Battle Creek, Mich.	67,725	43,453
Brookhaven, Miss.	10,820	8,220
Corpus Christi, Tex.	119,825	110,900
Frankfort, Ky.	16,535	11,916
Freeport, Ill.	24,637	22,467
Jacksonville, Ill.	22,600	20,600
Jefferson City, Mo.	26,000	23,200
Lincoln, Neb.	103,625	97,423
Sioux Falls, S. D.	55,000	51,000
Streator, Ill.	20,720	17,268
Williamsburg, Va.	7,150	3,500
Total Population	**474,637**	**409,947**

In each of these urban areas the population of the central city forms the largest part of the total population; however, each area contains an appreciable amount of development in the fringe territory. None of the urban areas here studied is typical of the extensive metropolitan areas surrounding our leading cities which usually consist of a central city and a cluster of suburban cities. Since this important type of urban area is not included and since the total number surveyed is admittedly small, the following analysis does not pretend to be based on an adequate sample. It is presented as a preliminary study until more data of this type is accumulated.

As in the preceding discussion, all statistical comparisons of land use data are based on the relationship of the amount of land in a particular use to the total developed area or to the population. Data obtained from the eleven land use surveys of urban areas are shown in Tables 9 and 10. For convenience, these data are also summarized in Table 11.

DEVELOPED AREAS

The total amount of land occupied by some form of urban use in the eleven urban areas is about 75 per cent greater than the sum of the developed areas of the eleven parent cities. The occupied land in the urban areas totals 70,440 acres, while for the central cities the total was 40,506 acres. In terms of population, the total developed area per 100 persons averages 14.84 acres for the eleven urban areas, but only 9.88 acres per 100 for the central cities. However, considering only that portion of the urban area outside the central city, the average use is 46.27 acres per 100 persons. As we will see later, this unusually high ratio for the fringe is due to the location in peripheral areas of numerous public and semipublic uses—airports, institutions, cemeteries, and some industries found on the outskirts of metropolitan areas.

The ratios of developed area to population found for the eleven urban areas range between 8.96 acres and 107.55 acres per 100 persons. Williamsburg, Va., possesses the unusually high ratio of 107.55;* the remaining ten cities range between 8.96 acres and 17.91 acres per 100 persons. The range for the parent cities of the eleven urban areas is from 7.37 acres to 32.28 acres per 100 persons. Historic Williamsburg, with its many public areas, again has the highest ratio of developed area to population, 32.28. Excluding Williamsburg, the range for the other ten cities is between 7.37 and 11.36 acres per 100 persons.

* It will be remembered that Williamsburg has a somewhat unique land use pattern. However, since it is a comparatively small city, its deviation from the norm has little effect on the group averages.

RESIDENTIAL AREAS

The residential uses occupy a slightly larger proportion of the urban area than any other use. An average of 27.99 per cent of the total developed area is so used. The proportions found in the eleven urban areas surveyed range between 7.55 per cent and 44.05 per cent of the developed areas. Williamsburg, Va., has the unusually low percentage of 7.55; the range for the other ten urban areas is from 21.09 per cent to 44.05 per cent. Residential uses in the eleven central cities that form the cores of these urban areas occupy 38.20 per cent of the total developed areas. This is about one-third more than the percentage for whole urban areas. There is less variation in the percentage of the developed area devoted to the residential use in the central cities. The range for the cities is between 20.30 per cent and 50.53 per cent.

Since the urban areas have appreciably less land in residential use than their main components, the central cities, the area beyond the city limits must be predominantly nonresidential. An examination of the fringe areas proves this to be true. On an average, only 14.18 per cent of the total developed area lying outside the central city is used for residential purposes. As will be seen later, the large demand on land in the fringe territory is for public and semipublic uses, thus reducing the proportion of land devoted to other uses.

The amount of land used for dwelling purposes in the eleven urban areas ranges between 3.07 acres and 8.12 acres per 100 persons. The low ratio is found in Sioux Falls, S. D., and the high ratio in Williamsburg, Va. The average use was found to be 4.16 acres per 100 persons. This is a higher ratio than that found in the eleven central cities, where only 3.77 acres per 100 persons is used for all residential purposes. The range is narrower in central cities, being between 2.91 acres and 6.56 acres per 100 persons. Thus, contrary to the fact that a substantially smaller percentage of total developed land is used in the urban area for dwelling purposes, a larger amount of land is used for each unit of the population. An analysis of that part of the urban area lying outside the central cities reveals that 6.57 acres per 100 persons are utilized for housing. The generous use of land in these fringe areas accounts for the larger average usage found in the complete urban areas.

SINGLE-FAMILY DWELLING AREAS

The single-family dwelling area occupies a greater proportion of the developed land than any other in the urban area. An average of 25.05 per cent of the total developed area is so used. The eleven urban areas surveyed have proportions ranging between 6.60 per cent and 38.64 per cent. The Williamsburg, Va. urban area devotes only 6.60 per cent of its total developed area to single-family use. The remaining ten urban areas have proportions between 19.65 per cent in Lincoln, Neb., and 38.64 per cent in Freeport, Ill. For comparison, the eleven cities use 33.34 per cent of their developed area for single-family dwelling purposes. The range found for the central cities is between 15.10 per cent in Williamsburg, Va., and 45.82 per cent of the total developed area in Streator, Ill. Again it is apparent that the area lying outside the central city has a small percentage of its land in dwellings and consequently, the average for the entire urban area is reduced below that of the city. The fringes of the eleven urban areas—or that portion outside the central cities—devote only 13.84 per cent of the developed area to single-family dwellings.

On the basis of population, the urban areas use 3.72 acres of land per 100 persons for single-family dwellings. The eleven central cities use somewhat less land for this purpose, or on an average 3.29 acres per 100 persons. A relatively wide range in ratios is found both for the urban areas and the central cities. Of the urban areas Sioux Falls, S. D., has the lowest ratio (2.67 acres) and Williamsburg, Va., the highest (7.10 acres). Frankfort, Ky., has the lowest ratio (1.99 acres per 100 persons) of the eleven central cities, and Brookhaven, Miss., the highest (4.93 acres).

TWO-FAMILY DWELLING AREAS

The two-family dwelling ranks second in use of land for residential purposes. In contrast with the large amount of land utilized by single-family dwellings, this subdivision of the dwelling area occupies only 1.63 per cent of the total developed area. However, only 0.20 per cent of the developed area lying outside the central city is in two-family usage. This low amount of two-family development in the fringe area reduces the percentage found in the urban area to 1.63; whereas, in the central cities 2.68 per cent of the developed area is so used. The range in proportion of land occupied by two-family dwellings in the eleven urban areas is between 0.21 per cent and 5.71 per cent of the total developed area. The range for the corresponding central cities is between 1.19 per cent and 8.00 per cent of the total developed area.

The eleven urban areas use an average of 0.24 acres of land per 100 persons for two-family dwellings. The range found is between 0.12 acres and 0.51 acres per population unit. Lincoln, Neb., has the low ratio and Frankfort, Ky., the high one. The ratio for the eleven central cities is slightly higher, or 0.26 acres per 100 persons. The range for the central cities is between 0.13 acres and 0.59 acres per 100 persons.

MULTIFAMILY DWELLING AREAS

Multifamily dwellings occupy a smaller proportion of the total dwelling area than either of the other two subdivisions, that is, only 4.69 per cent of the total dwelling area, and only 1.31 per cent of the total development of the eleven urban areas. The Streator, Ill., urban area has the lowest proportion of multifamily development, with 0.35 per cent of its developed area in this use. The urban area centering on Jacksonville, Ill., has the highest percentage of multifamily development, some 2.86 of its total developed area being so used.

The average for these urban areas is substantially lower than that found in the eleven central cities. The central cities have an average of 2.18 per cent of their developed area in multifamily use, compared with the 1.31 per cent found in the urban areas. This lower proportion for the entire urban area is due to the paucity of multifamily development in the fringe areas. Only 0.14 per cent of the urban area beyond the city limits is devoted to multifamily use. It is apparent that multifamily development in the urban areas studied is largely a central city activity; very little land is absorbed in peripheral areas by this use.

Only 0.20 acres of land per 100 persons is occupied by multifamily dwellings in the eleven urban areas. However, the range in ratios is between 0.05 acres and 0.80 acres per 100 persons. The Streator, Ill., urban area has the lowest ratio while the Williamsburg, Va., urban area has the highest. The ratios for the eleven corresponding cities are wider spread, ranging between 0.06 acres and 1.29 acres per 100 persons. These extremes for the cities are found in the same localities as those for the urban areas: Streator (where virtually no multifamily development exists outside the city boundaries) and Williamsburg. On an average, the central cities have approximately the same ratio as the eleven urban areas: 0.22 acres per 100 persons as compared with the 0.20 acres per 100 persons absorbed in the urban areas.

SUMMARY OF RESIDENTIAL USES

Each major residential use occupies a smaller percentage of the developed land in the eleven urban areas than it does within the corporate limits of its central city.

| | PERCENTAGE OF TOTAL DEVELOPED AREA | | | |
| | ELEVEN URBAN AREAS | | ELEVEN CENTRAL CITIES | |
RESIDENTIAL USE	AVERAGE	RANGE	AVERAGE	RANGE
Single-family dwellings	25.05	(6.60 – 38.64)	33.34	(15.10 – 45.82)
Two-family dwellings	1.63	(0.21 – 5.71)	2.68	(1.19 – 8.00)
Multifamily dwellings	1.31	(0.35 – 2.86)	2.18	(0.57 – 4.47)
Total residential	27.99	(7.55 – 44.05)	38.20	(20.30 – 50.53)

From this summary it can be seen that the percentage of total developed land used for residential purposes is about one-third less in the urban areas than in the central cities. Since the fringe territory is the natural location for various activities requiring large tracts of land—such as metropolitan parks, airports, schools, and institutions—proportionately less land in these areas is devoted to residential use. On an average, only 14.18 per cent of these fringe areas is occupied by residential developments: single-family dwellings occupy 13.84 per cent; two-family dwellings, 0.20 per cent; and multifamily dwellings, 0.14 per cent. Thus, viewed according to the land they occupy, residential uses are of secondary importance in the fringe area, a fact reflected in, and lowering, the percentage for the urban areas.

However, more land is used per unit of population for all residential purposes in the urban area than in the central cities. In these urban areas 4.16 acres per 100 persons is used for residential purposes compared to 3.77 acres per 100 persons in their central cities.

RESIDENTIAL USE	ACRES PER 100 PERSONS			
	ELEVEN URBAN AREAS		ELEVEN CENTRAL CITIES	
	AVERAGE	RANGE	AVERAGE	RANGE
Single-family dwellings	3.72	(2.67 – 7.10)	3.29	(1.99 – 4.93)
Two-family dwellings	0.24	(0.12 – 0.51)	0.26	(0.13 – 0.59)
Multifamily dwellings	0.20	(0.05 – 0.80)	0.22	(0.06 – 1.29)
Total residential	4.16	(3.07 – 8.12)	3.77	(2.91 – 6.56)

A study of the fringe territory outside the central cities shows that residential uses occupy 6.57 acres for each 100 persons in the population. It is this generous use of land per population that accounts for the larger ratio found for the complete urban areas. Few two-family and multifamily dwellings are found beyond the corporate limits. While single-family dwellings occupy 6.41 acres per 100 persons, two-family dwellings absorb 0.09 acres, and multifamily dwellings only 0.07 acres per 100 persons.

We now consider the land used for the various commercial, industrial, recreational, and public and semipublic activities found in the urban areas—uses that occupy almost three-fourths of the total developed area. In the study of these areas, we are dealing with the complex of activities that make up the modern American community. We are dealing with land uses that are typically central area activities, as well as with those that have developed special affinities for peripheral areas.

COMMERCIAL AREAS

Commercial uses in urban areas occupy 2.65 per cent of the total developed area, somewhat less than the 3.12 per cent utilized in the eleven central cities. The range in percentages for the eleven urban areas is between 1.15 per cent (Williamsburg, Va.) and 4.64 per cent (Battle Creek, Mich.) of the total developed area. This is about the same range found in the corresponding central cities. The eleven cities have percentages ranging from 1.78 in Lincoln, Neb., to 4.98 in Corpus Christi, Tex.

	PERCENTAGE OF TOTAL DEVELOPED AREA			
	ELEVEN URBAN AREAS		ELEVEN CENTRAL CITIES	
	AVERAGE	RANGE	AVERAGE	RANGE
Commercial uses	2.65	(1.15 – 4.64)	3.12	(1.78 – 4.98)

Again the land usage in the territory outside the central cities is substantially less than that found in the cities. In the case of commercial uses, only 2.01 per cent of the developed portion of the fringe territory is so used. This relatively low proportion when figured in with the percentage for the central cities reduces the mean for the total urban areas. In this respect, commercial uses are linked with residential uses; both occupy a smaller percentage of the total developed land in the urban areas than in their principle components, the central cities.

More land per unit of population is used for commercial purposes in the urban areas than in the central cities. Commercial uses occupy 0.39 acres of land for each 100 persons in the urban areas while 0.31 acres per 100 persons is so used in the cities. The range for the urban areas is between 0.24 acres and 1.23 acres per 100 persons. Frankfort, Ky., has the low ratio while Williamsburg, Va., has the unusually high ratio of 1.23. The ten other urban areas fall within a range of 0.24–0.59 acres per 100 persons.

	ACRES PER 100 PERSONS			
	ELEVEN URBAN AREAS		ELEVEN CENTRAL CITIES	
	AVERAGE	RANGE	AVERAGE	RANGE
Commercial uses	0.39	(0.24 – 1.23)	0.31	(0.19 – 1.47)

An average of 0.93 acres for commercial usage per 100 persons was found in the areas outside the central cities. This high ratio of commercial land to population reflects the centrifugal dispersion of commerce that has taken place within recent years. It points up, too, the fact that a growing share of the commercial activities is taking place outside the central business area—in outlying commercial centers that not only serve the adjacent residential areas, but also attract patrons from other parts of the city and frequently from quite a distance.

LIGHT INDUSTRY

An average of 1.87 per cent of the developed land in the eleven urban areas is devoted to light industry. This is substantially less than the proportion used for this purpose in the eleven corresponding central cities. On an average, these cities devote 2.42 per cent of their total developed areas to light industrial uses.

	PERCENTAGE OF TOTAL DEVELOPED AREA			
	ELEVEN URBAN AREAS		ELEVEN CENTRAL CITIES	
	AVERAGE	RANGE	AVERAGE	RANGE
Light industry	1.87	(0.69 – 4.00)	2.42	(1.52 – 4.99)

Again the low average for the urban areas results from the small amount of land used for light industry in the peripheral area. Of the developed land lying outside the central cities, only 1.13 per cent is occupied by light industry.

In terms of population, a slightly greater amount of land is used for light industry in the urban areas than in the central cities. Light industrial uses occupy 0.28 acres of land per 100 persons in the urban areas, compared to 0.24 acres in the central cities. However, in both cases there is a wide range in use between different cities or areas.

	ACRES PER 100 PERSONS			
	ELEVEN URBAN AREAS		ELEVEN CENTRAL CITIES	
	AVERAGE	RANGE	AVERAGE	RANGE
Light industry	0.28	(0.17 – 0.75)	0.24	(0.16 – 0.56)

Thus, of the eleven urban areas surveyed a much smaller percentage of land is devoted to light industry in the peripheral areas than in the central cities. However, with its relatively sparse population, more land per hundred persons is devoted to light industry in the fringe areas than in the city area.

HEAVY INDUSTRY

Heavy industry is traditionally associated with the routes of transportation, especially with railroads and harbors. While good transportation facilities remain a prime requisite for industrial sites and heavy industry continues to be located close to these services, new plants are moving outside congested areas, along main or belt lines. The result of this move to the fringe territory is noticeable when land uses for heavy industry are compared for the two components of the urban area.

In the eleven urban areas 3.77 per cent of the total developed land is occupied by heavy industry; whereas, in the central cities this use occupies only 2.52 per cent of the developed area. Thus, unlike light industries, heavy industrial processes predominate in the areas outside the central city. On an average, nearly 5.5 per cent. of the developed land in the fringe areas is devoted to heavy industry, or almost twice the proportion of that in the eleven central cities.

	PERCENTAGE OF TOTAL DEVELOPED AREA			
	ELEVEN URBAN AREAS		ELEVEN CENTRAL CITIES	
	AVERAGE	RANGE	AVERAGE	RANGE
Heavy industry	3.77	(0.11 – 12.50)	2.52	(0.51 – 5.72)

The proportion of the urban area that is devoted to heavy industrial uses varies considerably among cities. In the urban area centering on Williamsburg, Va., only 0.11 per cent of the developed area is occupied by heavy industry. At the other extreme, 12.50 per cent of the developed land in the Streator, Ill., urban area is devoted to this use. A greater variation is found in the proportions of heavy industrial use among the urban areas than in the central cities. The range for the eleven cities is between 0.51 per cent and 5.72 per cent of the total developed areas. The governmental center of Lincoln, Neb., possesses the lowest percentage, while Streator, Ill., has the highest.

The eleven urban areas are found to have 0.56 acres of heavy industrial development per 100 persons. The range is wide and varies between 0.08 acres and 1.79 acres per 100 persons. In land per population, the eleven central cities use less than half the amount used by urban areas. On an average, these cities devote 0.25 acres of land to this use for each 100 persons. The range for the central cities is narrower, varying between 0.05 acres (Lincoln, Neb.) and 0.60 acres (Streator, Ill.) per 100 persons. The averages and ranges for the urban areas and their central cities are shown in the following table.

	ACRES PER 100 PERSONS			
	ELEVEN URBAN AREAS		ELEVEN CENTRAL CITIES	
	AVERAGE	RANGE	AVERAGE	RANGE
Heavy industry	0.56	(0.08 – 1.79)	0.25	(0.05 – 0.60)

RAILROAD PROPERTY

The amount of land occupied by railroad property in the urban areas also varies greatly. The proportions range between 1.89 per cent of the total developed land in the Williamsburg, Va., urban area, and 11.63 per cent in the Lincoln, Neb., area. An average of

6.22 per cent of the developed land of the eleven urban areas is so used. In the·central cities, railroad property occupies only 4.73 per cent of the developed area. Corpus Christi, Tex., has the smallest percentage of railroad property with only 1.62 per cent of its developed area in this use. The city of Streator, Ill., with a proportion of 7.94 per cent, has the highest utilization.

	PERCENTAGE OF TOTAL DEVELOPED AREA			
	ELEVEN URBAN AREAS		ELEVEN CENTRAL CITIES	
	AVERAGE	RANGE	AVERAGE	RANGE
Railroad property	6.22	(1.89 – 11.63)	4.73	(1.62 – 7.94)

Thus railroad property, from the standpoint of land use, is a highly significant component of the urban pattern, occupying 8.23 per cent of the developed portion of the area outside the central city.

The urban areas have 0.92 acres per 100 persons developed in railroad facilities, or about twice the ratio found for the eleven central cities.

	ACRES PER 100 PERSONS			
	ELEVEN URBAN AREAS		ELEVEN CENTRAL CITIES	
	AVERAGE	RANGE	AVERAGE	RANGE
Railroad property	0.92	(0.23 – 2.07)	0.47	(0.14 – 0.83)

The common practice of locating classification yards and other terminal facilities in the outskirts of cities contributes to the large usage of land for this activity in peripheral areas.

COMBINED LIGHT AND HEAVY INDUSTRY AND RAILROADS

When all industrial uses and railroad property are combined, a better perspective is obtained of their place in the urban land pattern.

	PERCENTAGE OF TOTAL DEVELOPED AREA			
	ELEVEN URBAN AREAS		ELEVEN CENTRAL CITIES	
USE	AVERAGE	RANGE	AVERAGE	RANGE
Light industry	1.87	(0.69 – 4.00)	2.42	(1.52 – 4.99)
Heavy industry	3.77	(0.11 – 12.50)	2.52	(0.51 – 5.72)
Railroad property	6.22	(1.89 – 11.63)	4.73	(1.62 – 7.94)
Combined uses	11.86	(2.69 – 23.15	9.67	(4.07 – 15.43)

The combined uses demonstrate that appreciably more land is

used for industry and railroads in the urban areas than in the corresponding eleven central cities. The range for the urban areas is between 2.69 per cent (Williamsburg, Va.) and 23.15 per cent (Streator, Ill.) of the developed areas; however, in eight of the eleven areas surveyed, industrial and railroad uses take over 10 per cent of the developed area. The range for the central cities is between 4.07 per cent and 15.43 per cent; but, in this case, only five of the eleven cities have more than 10 per cent of their developed area occupied by industry and railroad facilities. The higher average for the combined uses in the urban areas is accounted for by the large areas of industrial and railroad property found in the fringe. These areas occupy almost 15 per cent of all developed land in the territory outside the central cities. The amount of land in combined industrial and railroad use varies considerably among both the urban areas and central cities studied. The affinity of heavy industrial and railroad facilities for fringe areas, and the siting factors peculiar to these activities, contribute to local variations which are usually independent of size and population.

Light industry, heavy industry and railroad property, each occupy more acres per population unit in the urban areas than in the eleven central cities. On an average the urban areas use 1.76 acres per 100 persons to 0.96 acres in the eleven cities. In the case of light industry, only a slightly higher ratio is found; however, both heavy industry and railroad facilities in urban areas occupy about twice the acreage per 100 persons found in central cities. These differences are shown in the following table.

	ACRES PER 100 PERSONS			
	ELEVEN URBAN AREAS		ELEVEN CENTRAL CITIES	
USE	AVERAGE	RANGE	AVERAGE	RANGE
Light industry	0.28	(0.17 – 0.75)	0.24	(0.16 – 0.56)
Heavy industry	0.56	(0.08 – 1.79)	0.25	(0.05 – 0.60)
Railroad property	0.92	(0.23 – 2.07)	0.47	(0.14 – 0.83)
Combined uses	1.76	(0.69 – 3.17)	0.96	(0.58 – 1.60)

The importance of fringe areas in meeting these needs for urban land is apparent from the summary above. While light industry is essentially a central city activity from the point of the amount of land occupied, the heavy industry, and railroads that serve the metropolis rely heavily on peripheral areas to meet their space requirements.

STREETS

Streets, alleys, and other public thoroughfares in urban areas occupy 27.61 per cent of the total developed area. In comparing the two component parts of urban areas, it is noted that proportionally less land is used for streets in the fringe areas than in the core cities. The amount of land occupied by streets in the areas beyond the city limits is 23.63 per cent of the developed area, which is lower than the percentages for the cities or the urban areas shown below.

	PERCENTAGE OF TOTAL DEVELOPED AREA			
	ELEVEN URBAN AREAS		ELEVEN CENTRAL CITIES	
	AVERAGE	RANGE	AVERAGE	RANGE
Streets	27.61	(11.66 – 41.35)	30.55	(17.08 – 42.15)

Of the eleven urban areas, Williamsburg, Va., has the lowest proportion of its developed area in streets (11.66 per cent) and Jefferson City, Mo. (41.35 per cent), the highest. However, the majority of cities have between 25 and 30 per cent of their developed areas in this use.

When the amount of land used for streets is related to population, the urban areas are found to use about one-third more acres per 100 persons than do the central cities.

	ACRES PER 100 PERSONS			
	ELEVEN URBAN AREAS		ELEVEN CENTRAL CITIES	
	AVERAGE	RANGE	AVERAGE	RANGE
Streets	4.10	(2.35 – 12.54)	3.02	(1.78 – 5.51)

Though, as shown in the table, the range for the urban areas is wide—from 2.35 acres to 12.54 acres per 100 persons—yet in all but the case of Williamsburg, Va., the ratios fall between 2.35 acres and 7.41 acres per 100 persons.

Streets, by occupying 27.61 per cent of the total developed area, absorb the largest amount of land of any single use in the urban areas. While slightly less land is used for streets in the area beyond the city limits, the urban areas as a whole show the same consistency in proportion of land devoted to streets as the central and satellite cities where the percentages are 28.10 and 27.67 respectively.

PARKS AND PLAYGROUNDS

Parks and playgrounds occupy 4.59 per cent of the total developed land of the eleven urban areas. This is a slightly higher percentage of land than the 4.25 per cent which was used for this purpose in the eleven central cities. Parks constitute 5.05 per cent of the developed land in the fringe areas outside the central cities, which accounts for the higher overall figure found for the urban areas.

	PERCENTAGE OF TOTAL DEVELOPED AREA			
	ELEVEN URBAN AREAS		ELEVEN CENTRAL CITIES	
	AVERAGE	RANGE	AVERAGE	RANGE
Parks and playgrounds	4.59	(0.04 – 8.93)	4.25	(0.26 – 9.83)

There is a great variation between communities as to the amount of land devoted to parks and playgrounds, with the urban areas having a slightly narrower range than the central cities.

Parks and playgrounds occupy 0.68 acres per 100 persons in the urban areas, and 0.41 acres per 100 persons in the corresponding central cities. In neither case, it will be noted, do the ratios meet the accepted standard for park areas of one acre per 100 persons. Lincoln, Neb., with 1.19 acres per 100 persons is the only community with a ratio exceeding this standard. Jefferson City, Mo., is the only central city exceeding the standard. It has 1.09 acres of park development per 100 persons.

	ACRES PER 100 PERSONS			
	ELEVEN URBAN AREAS		ELEVEN CENTRAL CITIES	
	AVERAGE	RANGE	AVERAGE	RANGE
Parks and playgrounds	0.68	(0.02 – 1.19)	0.42	(0.03 – 1.09)

PUBLIC AND SEMIPUBLIC PROPERTY

The most significant difference between the land use pattern for the central cities and that of their urban areas is in the amount of land used for public and semipublic activities. Where this land use occupied 14.21 per cent of the total developed area of the eleven central cities, 25.30 per cent of all developed land in the urban areas is so occupied.

	PERCENTAGE OF TOTAL DEVELOPED AREA			
	ELEVEN URBAN AREAS		ELEVEN CENTRAL CITIES	
	AVERAGE	RANGE	AVERAGE	RANGE
Public and semipublic property	25.30	(6.52 – 76.91)	14.21	(2.57 – 53.75)

Airports, large institutions, and cemeteries make public and semipublic uses the largest single use of land found outside of the eleven central cities. On an average, 40.30 per cent of the developed areas beyond the corporate limits is occupied by public and semipublic uses.

The range for the eleven urban areas is extremely wide: between 6.52 per cent and 76.91 per cent of the total developed area. Freeport, Ill., has the lowest proportion of public uses, and Williamsburg, Va., the highest. However, it will be remembered that Williamsburg is unique in the amount of land devoted to public use. The other ten urban areas have proportions ranging from 6.52 to 27.22 per cent of the developed areas. The range for the corresponding central cities is between 2.57 per cent and 53.75 per cent of the total developed area.

The urban areas have almost three times the amount of land in public and semipublic use per unit of population as do the eleven cities as shown in the following table.

	ACRES PER 100 PERSONS			
	ELEVEN URBAN AREAS		ELEVEN CENTRAL CITIES	
	AVERAGE	RANGE	AVERAGE	RANGE
Public and semipublic property	3.75	(0.66 – 82.72)	1.40	(0.27 – 17.35)

The proportion of the urban area devoted to public and semipublic uses per unit of population varies a great deal from community to community. In the urban area centering on Freeport, Ill., only 0.66 acres per 100 persons is in public or semipublic use, but in the Williamsburg, Va., area this use occupies 82.72 acres of land per 100 persons. Excluding Williamsburg, the range for the urban areas is between 0.66 acres and 4.29 acres per 100 persons. The range for the eleven central cities is between 0.27 acres (Streator, Ill) and 17.35 acres (Williamsburg, Va.) per 100 persons. If Williamsburg is removed from the group of central cities, the range is 0.27 to 2.69 acres per 100 persons.

SUMMARY OF USES

A greater percentage of the developed land in these urban areas is devoted to nonprivate use than to all private uses. When the areas

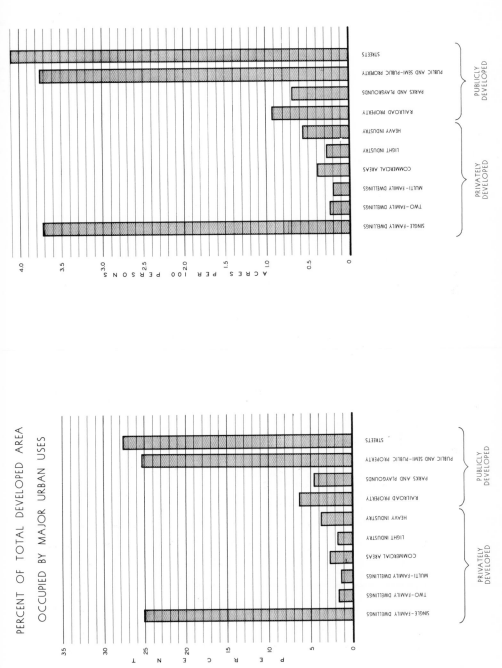

PLATE XIV. Land use in eleven urban areas

occupied by railroads, streets, parks, playgrounds, and other public and semipublic uses are summarized, it is found that an average of 63.72 per cent of the urban areas is so used with only 36.28 per cent devoted to private development.

	PERCENTAGE OF TOTAL DEVELOPED AREA	
	ELEVEN URBAN AREAS	ELEVEN CENTRAL CITIES
Privately developed property	36.28	46.26
Publicly developed property	63.72	53.74

The urban areas have a much larger proportion of their land in public development than do the other two groups studied: 63.72 per cent for urban areas compares with 53.74 per cent for their eleven central cities, 50.63 per cent for the fifty-three central cities, and only 47.62 per cent for the thirty-three satellite cities.

There is about one and one-half times as much developed land in the urban areas per unit of population as in the eleven central cities. Where in central cities the ratio of the amount of land used to population is about equally divided between public and private development, in the urban areas public development far outstrips private development.

	ACRES PER 100 PERSONS	
	ELEVEN URBAN AREAS	ELEVEN CENTRAL CITIES
Privately developed property	5.39	4.57
Publicly developed property	9.45	5.31
Total developed area	14.84	9.88

A comparison of all the uses of land in the eleven urban areas with those of their central cities is made in the following table, and shown graphically on Plate XIV.

	PERCENTAGE OF TOTAL DEVELOPED AREA	
USE	ELEVEN URBAN AREAS	ELEVEN CENTRAL CITIES
Single-family dwellings	25.05	33.34
Two-family dwellings	1.63	2.68
Multifamily dwellings	1.31	2.18
Commercial	2.65	3.12
Industrial and railroads	11.86	9.67
Streets	27.61	30.55
Parks and playgrounds	4.59	4.25
Public and semipublic property	25.30	14.21

In summary, there are wide variations among urban areas as to the amount of land used for each type of development. These differences arise from the social and economic forces at work in each community. Large differences are also found between the amount of land used for a given purpose in the central city and that used for the same purpose in its urban area. The reason for this is, of course, well known: the political city is seldom, if ever, a complete urban unit—complete as neither a social, nor an economic, nor a physical unit. A certain amount of the city's basic industry, for example, is located in the territory beyond the boundaries of the central city. Often the major recreational facilities of the metropolis are on the outskirts. An increasing amount of the city's daytime population lives beyond the city limits. Clearly, only in the urban area is there to be found a complete urban unit and only by analyzing the many uses of land throughout this area can the urban complex be comprehended.

6

CONCLUSIONS AND THEIR APPLICATIONS

Research can be concerned with establishing new principles, or with applying existing principles to new or emerging problems. The value of this work, it is hoped, lies in its contribution to both of these phases of research. Not only is it intended to provide data basic to the broader study of urban life, but it is also directed to practical application in urban planning and in the formulation of new zoning plans and the revision of existing ones.

Cities vary in size, in their social organization, in their economic activities, and in the number and type of institutions serving the inhabitants. They are in one way or another the products of numerous forces; as they grow and expand each develops an individuality of its own. On the other hand, different cities have many features in common. Each is, broadly speaking, a specialized part of our national social and industrial system. Each is, in varying degrees, a center of production and consumption of materials, goods and services, in which particular trades and activities tend to group together, and each contains the dwellings, institutions and amenities necessary for urban living.

Since the function of each city is in some respect different from that of all other cities, each tends to develop an individual and intricate pattern of land uses. Yet despite the dissimilarities the pattern of each is rational and essentially functional. In urban planning the real significance of land use data can be more easily appreciated when data for a large group of cities can be studied, and comparisons can be made between one type of land use and another. Extreme situations may appear in a limited number of cities. It is believed that the majority of conclusions valid for a diverse group of cities will apply, in appropriately modified form, to any city of approximately the same size. The value of these data is largely in their use in comparative analyses—in comparison between the various uses of urban land for different types and sizes of cities.

SUMMARY

In the foregoing chapters a detailed analysis has been presented of the amount of land utilized by the major urban activities. Land uses were analyzed separately for fifty-three central cities, thirty-three satellite cities, and eleven urban areas. In this chapter we have compiled the most important findings of the preceding analysis, and have made comparisons between the three basic groups studied: central cities, satellite cities, and urban areas. In the first two of these groups, the large number of cities included suggested that an analysis according to city size might be meaningful. For this reason the cities were grouped according to population. In some cases this grouping has pointed up significant correlations between populations and a type of land use; in other cases there is an obvious lack of correlation. The important relationships between city size and land use are mentioned in this summary chapter. Tables 3 and 4 contain the numerical data for central cities, analyzed by city size, and Tables 7 and 8 contain these data for the satellite cities.

There is a relationship between the total developed area of a city and the city's population. In central cities 6.89 acres of land per 100 persons is developed for some urban purpose. As the population increases, less area is proportionately required for urban development, until with the larger cities something of an equilibrium is reached. The same relationship is found for the satellite cities although, as a general rule, a larger amount of land is used in the satellite city per unit of population than in the central city. On an average there are 8.69 acres of urban development per 100 persons in suburban communities. From the survey of eleven urban areas, it seems clear that when the total urban pattern is considered the use of land per unit of population can be expected to be strikingly different. The urban area includes the land given over to the services and amenities necessary to sustain the metropolitan area. It includes, for example, the airports, metropolitan parks, and institutions that are typical fringe area activities although they serve the entire metropolitan community. The amount of developed land in the urban areas is 14.84 acres per 100 persons—or twice the development per unit of population found in the central city.

It is in the division of this developed land among the ten major types of development that we are primarily interested.

	PERCENTAGE OF TOTAL DEVELOPED AREA		
USE	FIFTY-THREE CENTRAL CITIES	THIRTY-THREE SATELLITE CITIES	ELEVEN URBAN AREAS
Single-family dwellings	31.81	36.18	25.05
Two-family dwellings	4.79	3.31	1.63
Multifamily dwellings	3.01	2.49	1.31
Commercial areas	3.32	2.54	2.65
Light industry	2.84	7.86*	1.87
Heavy industry	3.60		3.77
Railroad property	4.86	4.65	6.22
Streets	28.19	27.67	27.61
Parks and playgrounds	6.74	4.37	4.59
Public and semipublic property	10.93	10.93	25.30
Total developed area	100.00	100.00	100.00

Data compiled for these ten classifications have been treated in two different ways: the amount of land has been figured as a percentage of the total developed area and as a ratio to each 100 persons of the population. The preceding table shows the percentages, and the following table the ratios for each type of land development for the central cities, satellite cities, and urban areas.

	ACRES PER 100 PERSONS		
USE	FIFTY-THREE CENTRAL CITIES	THIRTY-THREE SATELLITE CITIES	ELEVEN URBAN AREAS
Single-family dwellings	2.19	3.14	3.72
Two-family dwellings	0.33	0.29	0.24
Multifamily dwellings	0.21	0.22	0.20
Commercial areas	0.23	0.22	0.39
Light industry	0.20	0.69*	0.28
Heavy industry	0.25		0.56
Railroad property	0.33	0.40	0.92
Streets	1.94	2.40	4.10
Parks and playgrounds	0.46	0.38	0.68
Public and semipublic property	0.75	0.95	3.75
Total developed area	6.89	8.69	14.84

* Light and heavy industry were combined in the case of satellite cities because for a number of cities the classifications were combined in the original survey.

Data from these two tables will be discussed in the following paragraphs. It is opportune to point out again here, however, that the percentages and the ratios have meanings quite different from each other. By definition, one relates to the total developed area, and the other to the population. In comparing the figures for the three groups studied, the relative importance of the different groups is often reversed. For example, in single-family housing, the percentage of total developed area for urban areas is much lower than for central or satellite cities. What single-family housing does exist, however, is located on much more generous land sites in urban areas than in the other groups. As a result the ratio of acres per hundred persons is considerably higher for the urban areas than for the cities. It is clear that the reversed order of size between the percentages and ratios for the three groups implies no contradiction.

Residential Areas. A greater portion of the developed area of cities is devoted to residential use than to any other use. In central cities the residential area occupies 39.61 per cent of the total developed land. As might be expected, an even larger portion of satellite cities is used for dwelling purposes: 41.98 per cent of the developed areas of the thirty-three cities surveyed were found to be in some residential use. However, in the urban areas there is a decrease in the percentage of developed land for residential use and a corresponding increase in the nonresidential use. In the urban areas the residential uses occupy only 27.99 per cent of the developed area.

The areas used for dwelling purposes, when expressed in terms of acres per 100 persons, show a relationship according to size of population. The larger cities have fewer acres of dwelling area per unit of population than have the smaller cities. Thus it can be said that the amount of land used for dwelling purposes varies inversely with the population. On an average, the central cities use 2.73 acres and the satellite cities use 3.65 acres per 100 persons. It was found in the case of urban areas that 4.16 acres per 100 persons was utilized for dwellings. Thus, we find that while a substantially smaller percentage of the total developed land in the urban area is in residential use, due to the progressively decreasing densities found as urban development spreads out, a larger amount of land is used for each unit of the population.

Single-Family Dwelling Areas. The area used for single-family dwellings is the largest subdivision of the total dwelling area. In central cities this use occupies 31.81 per cent of the total developed area. Smaller cities tend to devote a somewhat greater proportion of their developed areas to this use, and large cities (where high densities prevail), a smaller proportion. The single-family dwelling areas in satellite cities occupy 36.18 per cent of the developed land. But in the urban areas surveyed only 25.05 per cent of the developed area is occupied by this subdivision of the dwelling area. Thus the average city uses about one-third of its developed area for single-family housing, but only one-fourth of the urban area is so used as a general rule.

There is also an apparent relationship between the population of the city and the acreage ratios of single-family dwelling areas to population. In the central cities surveyed an average of 2.19 acres per 100 persons is used for single-family dwellings. Larger cities on a whole have lower ratios while the smaller cities tend to have higher and more variable ratios. This is also true of the satellite cities; however, the smaller satellite cities have considerably higher ratios than the larger cities. On an average, suburban cities devote 3.14 acres of land per 100 persons to single-family dwellings. From the urban areas surveyed, it would seem that the more generous usage of land for dwelling purposes in the outskirts brings up the rather low acreage ratios in the core areas, for an average of 3.72 acres of land per 100 persons is found for the urban areas. This is, of course, only about one-half acre more land per 100 persons than used in the satellite cities.

Two-Family Dwelling Areas. The two-family dwelling ranks second in popularity as a housing structure. However, in contrast with the large areas utilized for single-family dwellings, only a comparatively small portion of the total developed area is in two-family use. In the central cities this proportion is 4.79 per cent, and in the satellite cities 3.31 per cent, of the developed area. In the study of urban areas it was found that in the unincorporated territory outside of the central cities only 0.20 per cent of the developed land was devoted to two-family dwellings, and only 1.63 per cent of the developed portions of the entire urban areas was so used. Thus, we find that the two-family dwellings are more prevalent in the central city and are found in lessening numbers the farther a given area is from the core of the metropolis. Lastly, the two-family dwellings are found to be favored more in the eastern cities studied than in other regions, and in all cases they are more commonly found in larger cities than in smaller ones. On an average, the central cities use 0.33 acres per 100 persons for two-family dwelling whereas the satellite cities use 0.29 acres per 100 persons. In the eleven urban areas surveyed, only 0.24 acres per 100 persons was developed in two-family dwellings. Thus, in generalization, it seems reasonable to say that the two-family dwelling area will occupy a relatively small proportion of the total dwelling area in any given city, seldom exceeding 5 per cent of the developed area. However, there seems to be little relationship between the land so used per 100 persons and the total population. Regardless of the size of city, it is found that from about one-fourth to one-third of an acre of land is absorbed per 100 persons for this use.

Multifamily Dwelling Areas. The multifamily dwelling has long been associated with areas of concentration and high land values. The apartment is still, of course, indigenous to the larger cities; however, it is no longer confined to central areas, but is found increasingly in suburban communities. In central cities 3.01 per cent of the total developed area is devoted to multifamily dwellings, while in the suburban cities 2.49 per cent of the developed area is used for this purpose. The average for the urban areas studied is 1.31 per cent.*

There is an apparent relationship between the size of city and the amount of land per unit of population used for multifamily buildings. Unlike the case of the single-family dwelling area (where the ratio diminishes as the population increases), in multifamily use it is found that the larger the city, the greater the ratio of land used to population. On an average the central cities use 0.21 acres for this purpose per 100 persons of the population. The same relationship is observed in the suburban cities where 0.22 acres per 100 persons is used for multifamily dwellings. In the urban areas the ratio of land used to population is 0.20 acres per 100 persons.

* It should be remembered that most of the eleven urban areas studied are medium or small in size and their land use patterns, therefore, are not comparable in all cases to the other cities surveyed.

XV. Multifamily housing. Above, the ubiquitous city apartment; below, Hancock Village garden-type apartments, Boston, Mass. Lower photograph courtesy of The Urban Land Institute

The future trend in multifamily housing construction is obscure. The apartment house has been accepted by a large number of people as an efficient, if not altogether satisfactory, domicile in metropolitan areas. Under government sponsorship we are seeing the construction of new apartment groups in peripheral areas and the absorption of proportionately more urban land by these projects of relatively low population density. Yet unless the trend to the apartment increases more than is foreseeable at the present time, or unless it is sustained by economic conditions over a long period of time, there seems to be little reason to expect multifamily dwellings to occupy more than a relatively small percentage of the developed urban land.

Summary of All Residential Uses. When all three residential uses are combined, a better understanding of their relative proportions is realized.

	PERCENTAGE OF TOTAL DEVELOPED AREA		
TYPE OF USE	FIFTY-THREE CENTRAL CITIES	THIRTY-THREE SATELLITE CITIES	ELEVEN URBAN AREAS
Single-family dwellings	31.81	36.18	25.05
Two-family dwellings	4.79	3.31	1.63
Multifamily dwellings	3.01	2.49	1.31
Total residential	39.61	41.98	27.99

In both the central cities and suburban cities about two-fifths of the developed land is devoted to residential use. From the urban areas surveyed we find that the portion of the developed land devoted to dwellings is less when the entire urban area is considered —about one-fourth of the developed land in the urban areas being in residential use.

Commercial Areas. To turn to the nonresidential uses of urban land, we find that a substantial amount of all developed urban land is devoted to commercial, industrial, recreational, and public and semipublic uses. These uses provide the economic lifeblood of the community, and the necessary services and amenities for urban living.

Of these uses, commercial activities are particularly important to the economic life of the community. The amount of land in this use tends to fluctuate with general economic conditions, and in times of prosperity overoptimism, together with the relative ease of starting commercial enterprises, sometimes results in unwarranted

XVI. Commercial development. The contrast between the new integrated shopping center with off-street parking facilities and the "string"
development above is vivid. Lower photograph courtesy of River Oaks
Corporation, Houston, Texas

demands for commercial lands. These demands lead to the over-exploitation of urban land for commercial purposes and as a result many early zoning plans erroneously provided seemingly unlimited areas for commercial expansion. In fact, relatively little land is used for commercial purposes and there is an optimum amount that can be absorbed by this use for a given population. The average amount of land used for commercial purposes in central cities is 3.32 per cent of the total developed area. There is a trend for the percentage of area devoted to commerce to increase as the size of the city increases. However, from the study of satellite cities, where an average of 2.54 per cent of the developed area is so used, it is found that factors such as travel distances to major commercial centers, social status, and family income all modify the local demands for commercial space. If the entire urban area is considered, the commercial areas are found to occupy a somewhat smaller percentage of the developed land. On an average, this use of urban land is found to absorb 2.65 per cent of the developed portion of urban areas.

Central cities devote 0.23 acres and satellite cities 0.22 acres of land per 100 persons to commercial use. The ratio for the entire metropolitan community is higher. In the eleven urban areas the ratio of commercial land to population is 0.39 acres per 100 persons. Thus while the greatest concentration of commercial uses are in the central areas, dispersion in outlying areas accounts for a considerable part of the total commercial area in the community.

Light Industry. The light industrial area has in the past centered on the central business districts of the city.* Many light industries are ancillary to the activities of the business district and are properly located in close proximity to it. Others do not have this economic tie and are found scattered in various sections of the city and in peripheral areas. By and large, however, light industry tends to be a central area activity to which central cities devote 2.84 per cent of their total developed areas. In the urban areas, only 1.87 per cent of the total developed land is so used. The actual amount of land devoted to light industrial uses in a given community varies, of course, in accordance with the character of

---

* Comparisons are made between central cities and urban areas only, since this classification has been combined with heavy industry in the case of satellite cities.

the city and its tributary region. All cities contain some light industry to serve local needs; however, cities with industry serving broader regional or national markets must devote a greater proportion of their land resources to this use. Therefore, it is found that the proportionate amount of land in light industries varies greatly between cities, and in general, there is little relationship between land absorbed for this purpose and the population. The ratio of industrial land to population is 0.20 acres per 100 persons for the central cities, with the smaller cities tending to have higher ratios than larger cities. Among the urban areas surveyed, most of which were small communities, the average use was 0.28 acres per 100 persons.

Heavy Industry. The location of heavy industry in a municipality depends upon factors that are economic in nature, and that are local as well as national in scope. Chief among these are the availability of the materials of manufacture, sources of power, communications, and markets. A wide range is found between cities of approximately the same population in the amount of land devoted to heavy industry; however, proportionately more land is occupied by this use in large cities than in small cities. On an average 3.60 per cent of the developed area of central cities is given over to heavy industry. The prevalence of heavy industry in fringe areas raises the percentage when the entire urban area is considered. From the survey of eleven urban areas it is found that 3.77 per cent of the developed land is used by heavy industry. Since these urban areas are all comparatively small communities, a greater percentage is probable in large metropolitan centers. The average use for the central cities is 0.25 acres per 100 persons with 0.56 acres per 100 persons in the urban areas. In both cases wide ranges are found between individual communities. There seems to be little or no relationship between the amount of land per population utilized by heavy industry and the size of the community.

Railroad Property. An even greater variation is found in the proportion of the developed area devoted to railroad facilities in different cities. Since the amount of railroad property is conditioned by external as well as local factors, there is little uniformity between the land so used in cities of approximately the same size. On an average, however, central cities devote 4.86 per cent of their

PLATE XVII. Industrial plants. The change from the multistory struct
horizontal plants with nuisance control devices, air conditionin
street parking, and landscaped sites is altering the land use patte
requires rethinking of use classifications. Lower photograph court
Chrysler Airtemp, Division of Chrysler Corp.

developed area to railroad facilities, while 4.65 per cent is the average for satellite cities. The location of terminal facilities in the outskirts of metropolitan areas accounts for greater land requirements in the urban areas. From the survey of the eleven urban areas it is found that this use occupies 6.22 per cent of the developed land. In relation to population, railroads used 0.33 acres per 100 persons in central cities, 0.40 acres in satellite cities, and 0.92 acres in urban areas.

Combined Light and Heavy Industry and Railroads. When light and heavy industry and railroads are combined, a better perspective is obtained of their place in the urban land pattern. In central cities these combined uses absorb 11.30 per cent of the total developed area, or an average of 0.78 acres per 100 persons. Satellite cities use somewhat more land for these purposes—12.51 per cent of the total developed area, or 1.09 acres per 100 persons. The average for the eleven urban areas is 11.86 per cent of the total developed area, or 1.76 acres per 100 persons. There are wide variations between cities of approximately the same size and therefore no relationship can be assumed between the variables of land used and population. The amount of land used for these purposes will vary according to each city's needs and characteristics.

Streets. The second largest use of urban land is streets, alleys, highways and other public thoroughfares. In the central and satellite cities as well as the urban areas there is a relatively constant relationship between the street area and the total developed area. On an average, central cities devote 28.10 per cent of their developed area to this use while satellite cities use 27.67 per cent of their developed area for this purpose. In urban areas the average is 27.61 per cent of the total developed area. Moreover, the proportion of land used for streets in most cities falls within a relatively narrow range. Expressed in terms of population, central cities devote 1.94 acres of land to streets for each 100 persons in the population. Satellite cities have a higher ratio for street area, 2.40 acres per 100 persons. The large number of streets found in otherwise undeveloped peripheral areas gives the urban areas a much higher ratio. In the eleven urban areas, an average of 4.10 acres per 100 persons are found to be in streets and other public thoroughfares. In general, smaller cities use a greater percentage of their developed area for streets and also use more land per unit of population for this purpose than do larger cities.

Parks and Playgrounds. In central cities parks and playgrounds occupy 6.74 per cent of the developed area. In satellite cities, the average is 4.37 per cent of the total developed area. When the total urban area is considered, the average is slightly higher, or 4.59 per cent of the developed area. In all cases, however, a wide range is found in the percentages for individual communities, and there is no overall pattern or consistent variation according to city size. When the existing ratios of land devoted to parks and playgrounds are measured against the accepted planning standard of one acre of land for each 100 persons, few communities are found that meet this standard. On an average central cities have 0.46 acres of park and playground development per 100 persons, or less than half the desirable ratio. Satellite cities devote even less land to this purpose, or 0.38 acres per 100 persons. Outlying parks increase the ratios found for urban areas. On an average, the eleven urban areas have 0.68 acres of park and playground development per 100 persons.

Public and Semipublic Property. The most significant difference between the land use pattern for the central city and urban areas is in the amount of land used for public and semipublic activities. In central cities, and in satellite cities also, this use of urban land occupies 10.93 per cent of the total developed area. Over twice this proportion is used in urban areas where airports, institutions, cemeteries, and other public and semipublic uses combined occupy 25.30 per cent of the developed area. On an average over 40 per cent of the developed areas beyond the corporate limits is occupied by this type of land use. The proportion of the urban area devoted to public and semipublic uses per unit of population varies greatly from community to community. However, when the averages are considered, central cities are found to have 0.75 acres of public and semipublic development per 100 persons. Satellite cities devote 0.95 acres per 100 persons to this use. The urban areas on the other hand have five times as much public and semipublic development as the central cities per unit of population. The eleven areas surveyed contain 3.75 acres of this development per 100 persons. Small cities devote proportionally more land to public and semipublic uses than large cities. This is apparent in both central and

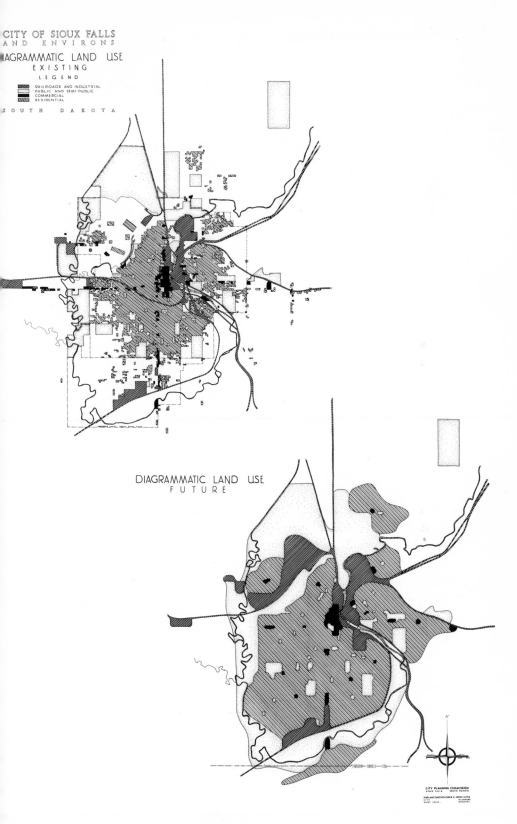

PLATE XVIII. Sioux Falls, South Dakota. Existing and proposed
land use plan

satellite cities, in percentages of developed area and in ratios to population.

Summary of Uses. In summary, a large proportion of the city and total urban area is devoted to nonprivate purposes. The area devoted to the major nonprivate uses of urban land—railroads, streets, parks and playgrounds, and public and semipublic uses— occupies 50.63 per cent of the developed land in the central city. Less than half of the developed land, 47.62 per cent, is used for these purposes in the satellite city. When the total urban areas are considered it is found that nonprivate development absorbs 63.72 per cent of all urban land.

	PERCENTAGE OF TOTAL DEVELOPED AREA		
	FIFTY-THREE CENTRAL CITIES	THIRTY-THREE SATELLITE CITIES	ELEVEN URBAN AREAS
Privately developed property	49.37	52.38	36.28
Publicly developed property	50.63	47.62	63.72

In cities the amount of land developed for each of these two divisions per unit of population is about equal. Urban areas use relatively more land per 100 persons for public development

	ACRES PER 100 PERSONS		
	FIFTY-THREE CENTRAL CITIES	THIRTY-THREE SATELLITE CITIES	ELEVEN URBAN AREAS
Privately developed property	3.41	4.56	5.39
Publicly developed property	3.48	4.13	9.45
Total developed	6.89	8.69	14.84

It is evident that there are wide variations in the land use patterns of the three components of the metropolitan area. In a sense, each unit—the central city, satellite city, and the urban fringe—is a specialized part of the entire urban area. Each community uses its land resources in a uniquely different way. This is manifest in the wide variety of land usage patterns found in a study of this type.

APPLICATIONS

This research discloses that there are definite limits to the amounts of land which will be used for various purposes. Since absolute amounts of land are not comparable for cities of varying sizes and populations, all land areas were discussed in terms of percentage

PLATE XIX. Washington, D. C. Existing and proposed land use plan

of developed area and ratios per 100 persons. In the case of certain uses, these ratios and percentages are fairly constant regardless of the size of the city or its geographical position. Where this is the case, the mean, or group averages which have been found from this data and recorded throughout the text, may be considered norms, or definite laws of absorption. A limited range above and below these norms will describe this use in all cities except a few where extreme conditions prevail. Among the use categories whose averages can be considered norms are residential areas, commercial areas, and streets. A constant pattern of land use is to be expected in these classifications where the demand for land is predicated on local factors.

Other types of land use which are founded on political as well as economic considerations, or which have an economic base extending beyond the local area, would not be expected to show a consistent pattern in the various cities. This is indeed the case. Great variations exist between cities in land used for light industry, heavy industry, railroad property, parks and playgrounds, and public and semipublic property. While a study of the data for these classifications reveals very broad limits which are likely to stand, the averages are not typical of enough cities to be considered norms or definite laws of absorption.

With each of the ten types of land uses, however, the comparative analyses made possible by the use of data from this study, together with supplementary local information, provide a reasonably reliable means of forecasting the future use of land in a community.

If zoning is to reach its highest and best form in encouraging and insuring the rational and economic development of urban land, it must be related to the amount of land that can be reasonably expected to be absorbed for various uses. Briefly, the specific application of these data and conclusions, in the preparation of new zoning plans and ordinances or in the revision of those now in force, may be made in the following manner.

The first step is the detailed survey of the character and extent of present urban development. The present development expressed in terms of acres per 100 persons can be calculated from this survey and, by comparing this ratio with that for similar cities, it is possible to arrive at a satisfactory norm for the future growth of the

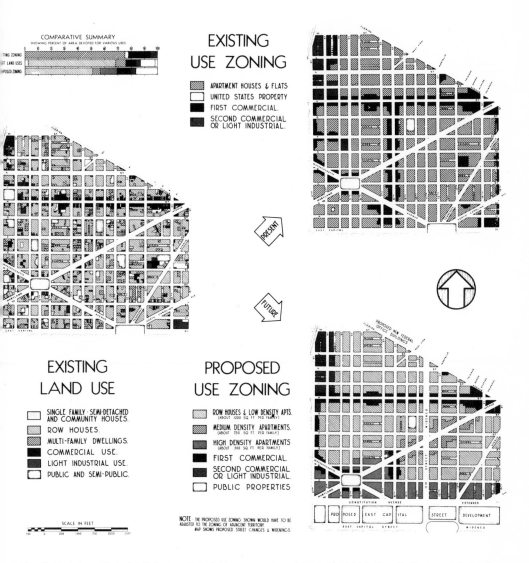

COMPARATIVE SUMMARY
SHOWING PERCENT OF AREA DEVOTED FOR VARIOUS USES

EXISTING ZONING
PRESENT LAND USES
PROPOSED ZONING

EXISTING USE ZONING

APARTMENT HOUSES & FLATS
UNITED STATES PROPERTY
FIRST COMMERCIAL.
SECOND COMMERCIAL OR LIGHT INDUSTRIAL.

PRESENT

FUTURE

EXISTING LAND USE

SINGLE FAMILY · SEMI-DETACHED AND COMMUNITY HOUSES.
ROW HOUSES.
MULTI-FAMILY DWELLINGS.
COMMERCIAL USE.
LIGHT INDUSTRIAL USE.
PUBLIC AND SEMI-PUBLIC.

PROPOSED USE ZONING

ROW HOUSES & LOW DENSITY APTS. (ABOUT 1200 SQ FT PER FAMILY)
MEDIUM DENSITY APARTMENTS. (ABOUT 150 SQ FT PER FAMILY)
HIGH DENSITY APARTMENTS (ABOUT 300 SQ FT PER FAMILY)
FIRST COMMERCIAL.
SECOND COMMERCIAL OR LIGHT INDUSTRIAL.
PUBLIC PROPERTIES

SCALE IN FEET

NOTE - THE PROPOSED USE ZONING SHOWN WOULD HAVE TO BE ADJUSTED TO THE ZONING OF ADJACENT TERRITORY
MAP SHOWS PROPOSED STREET CHANGES & WIDENINGS

NATIONAL CAPITAL PARK AND PLANNING COMMISSION

Area shown is in northeast Washington, north of proposed East Capitol Street development. Present uses are mixed. Present zoning provides for excessive commercial frontage and no population density control. Proposed zoning would retain the commercial center along H Street but reduce frontage for business along Eighth and Fifteenth Streets. Three types of multifamily zones would be included. Reduction in commercial and industrial zones would provide more effective control over location of these uses in the neighborhood.

PLATE XX. Washington, D. C. Example of proposed zoning revisions

city under consideration. An extrapolation of the land use for a future date, say 1980, can be made by applying this local norm to the figure of estimated future population.

Next, a tentative zoning plan should be prepared, the greatest care being taken to allocate areas for the different uses in accordance with the present pattern of conditions and providing for the future growth of various uses in the most appropriate locations. The amount of land assigned to the various land uses in the tentative zoning plan should be computed separately by districts and summarized for the entire city or urban area. The reasonableness of the tentative plan can be tested by relating it to the various norms discussed above and to estimates of the maximum area which will be absorbed by the various uses. The test for reasonableness should be applied to the total area of development as well as to local areas, so that necessary readjustments can then be made. These adjustments will, of course, be compatible with the several elements of the comprehensive plan.

The application of the results of this research to cities or urban areas in which zoning ordinances are now in effect, can follow much the same procedure. The field survey is the prime requisite. This should be followed by computations for the various areas now in use and supported by supplementary information on the social and economic characteristics of the community. Next, this information should be compared with the data on the areas actually provided for the various uses under the existing zoning plan; and finally, the existing plan should be adjusted to comply as nearly as possible with the actual land use requirements of the estimated future population. A comparison of this type is shown in Table 12.

The problem of changing the existing zoning plan and ordinance is much more difficult than the preparation of a new ordinance. The fact that the municipality has designated certain areas for specific uses has not only fixed their future use to a certain extent in the minds of property owners and citizens, but in some cases it has influenced land values. To change an existing ordinance requires patience and considerable effort. Satisfactory readjustments can be obtained as a rule only when the citizens completely understand the need for the change. However, some change must be made in many existing zoning ordinances if all

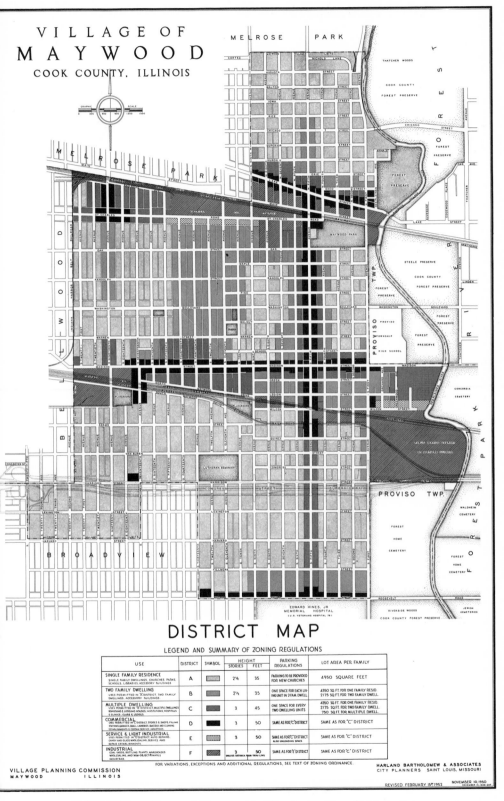

DISTRICT MAP

LEGEND AND SUMMARY OF ZONING REGULATIONS

USE	DISTRICT	SYMBOL	HEIGHT		PARKING REGULATIONS	LOT AREA PER FAMILY
			STORIES	FEET		
SINGLE FAMILY RESIDENCE SINGLE FAMILY DWELLINGS, CHURCHES, PARKS, SCHOOLS, LIBRARIES, ACCESSORY BUILDINGS.	A		2½	35	PARKING TO BE PROVIDED FOR NEW CHURCHES	4950 SQUARE FEET
TWO FAMILY DWELLING USES PERMITTED IN "A" DISTRICT, TWO FAMILY DWELLINGS, ACCESSORY BUILDINGS.	B		2½	35	ONE SPACE FOR EACH LIVING UNIT IN 2 FAM. DWELL.	4350 SQ. FT. FOR ONE FAMILY RESID. 2175 SQ.FT. FOR TWO FAMILY DWELL.
MULTIPLE DWELLING USES PERMITTED IN "B" DISTRICT, MULTIPLE DWELLINGS, BOARDING & LODGING HOUSES, INSTITUTIONS, HOSPITALS & CLINICS, CLUBS & LODGES.	C		3	45	ONE SPACE FOR EVERY TWO DWELLING UNITS	4350 SQ.FT. FOR ONE FAMILY RESID. 2175 SQ.FT. FOR TWO FAMILY DWELL. 750 SQ. FT. FOR MULTIPLE DWELL.
COMMERCIAL USES PERMITTED IN "C" DISTRICT, STORES & SHOPS, FILLING STATIONS, GARAGES, SMALL LAUNDRIES, BAKERIES AND CLEANING ESTABLISHMENTS & CUSTOM SERVICE INDUSTRIES.	D		3	50	SAME AS FOR "C" DISTRICT	SAME AS FOR "C" DISTRICT
SERVICE & LIGHT INDUSTRIAL USES PERMITTED IN "D" DISTRICT, AUTO REPAIRS, DAIRY AND GLASS WHOLESALING, SERVICE AND REPAIR ESTABLISHMENTS.	E		3	50	SAME AS FOR "C" DISTRICT ALSO UNLOADING SPACE	SAME AS FOR "C" DISTRICT
INDUSTRIAL COAL YARDS, BOTTLING PLANTS, WAREHOUSES, WHOLESALING, AND NON-OBJECTIONABLE INDUSTRIES.	F		3 UNLESS SETBACK FROM YARD LINE	50	SAME AS FOR "E" DISTRICT	SAME AS FOR "C" DISTRICT

FOR VARIATIONS, EXCEPTIONS AND ADDITIONAL REGULATIONS, SEE TEXT OF ZONING ORDINANCE.

VILLAGE PLANNING COMMISSION
MAYWOOD   ILLINOIS

HARLAND BARTHOLOMEW & ASSOCIATES
CITY PLANNERS   SAINT LOUIS, MISSOURI

REVISED FEBRUARY 15TH 1952

NOVEMBER 10, 1950

PLATE XXI. Village of Maywood, Illinois. Zoning district map

areas of the city are to be given the chance to maintain or improve their character and value.

Whether the problem is changing the existing zoning ordinance, or formulating a completely new plan, it is worth while to stress once again the vital importance of comprehensive planning. Brick, steel, and mortar once in place are difficult to alter. Urban planning means arranging the physical surroundings of people for generations in the future. Such vital determinations can be justified only if it is certain that every effort has been made to consider all the factors relevant to urbanization. In this, planning must be cognizant of the necessity for further research. If planning is to have adequate tools with which to work it must also assume leadership in the study of urbanism.

Seldom can we project our thinking into the future without building on the past. A thorough knowledge of the history, the habits, and the aspirations of urban society is a requisite to rational planning. It is well to remember that ours is a dynamic society and that we are seeing constant changes which require new appraisals and evaluations. Planning and zoning must cope with social changes, technological changes, and others, including strategic military considerations. The long-term effects of each of these factors must be considered in relation to their influence on the community.

Over and above this, it is worth remembering that in practice planning research must be directed toward establishing new principles or modifying existing principles to fit new needs. In zoning, for example, we need new and better means of classifying land uses. Particularly is there a need for revising industrial classifications to recognize new processes in which nuisances, commonly associated with certain industries in the early days of zoning, no longer exist due to improved techniques and controls. Scientifically determined performance standards offer great possibilities in evolving and enforcing zoning ordinances. More work must be done on the problem of nonconforming uses—incongruous uses that actually occupy little land but are serious hindrances to sound community development. A limited "life" should be imposed on these uses to assure that the use will be discontinued after a reasonable time has been allowed to amortize the original capital investment. To do otherwise, to create and protect special privileges and monopolies by legal sanction, is not in the best interests of the community and is contrary to democratic processes. Furthermore, it serves to penalize those who must observe the zoning plan.

There is urgent need for some solution to the growing administrative dilemma which urban planning faces. We have seen in preceding chapters that large metropolitan areas are mosaics of governmental units. Primarily political entities, these separate administrative units are poorly integrated into the geographic, cultural, institutional, and economic realities of the urban area. It is not our purpose here to belabor the cause of metropolitan unity. However, in the last few years experience has shown that whether the governmental structure is viewed from above, on the state or federal level, or from its relation to the people served, a larger and more logically defined unit is desirable. This is particularly true when planning and zoning are considered. Our cities are expanding laterally and many of the economic and technical ties that bound the population to a relatively small area are disappearing. As has been shown, land use patterns found in urban areas have little relationship to existing arbitrary boundaries. It seems reasonable to say that a land use plan can be realistically applied to best advantage where its coverage includes the whole urban area. It follows that zoning and planning are most effective when their span of control is comprehensive. Furthermore, the more complex the urban organization the greater the need for more careful control of land utilization.

APPENDICES

LIST OF CITIES SURVEYED WITH YEARS OF SURVEY

CENTRAL CITIES

Atchison, Kansas	1941	Memphis, Tennessee	1939
Bar Harbor, Maine	1947	Mexico, Missouri	1952
Baton Rouge, Louisiana	1946	Muskogee, Oklahoma	1945
Battle Creek, Michigan	1947	Naples, Florida	1952
Binghamton, New York	1948	Newark, New Jersey	1945
Brookhaven, Mississippi	1950	Oklahoma City, Oklahoma	1945
Carlsbad, New Mexico	1945	Petersburg, Virginia	1943
Centralia, Illinois	1940	Portsmouth, Virginia	1946
Corpus Christi, Texas	1951	Quincy, Illinois	1945
Davenport, Iowa	1945	Racine, Wisconsin	1938
Dallas, Texas,	1944	Richmond, Virginia	1942
Dayton, Ohio	1952	Rock Island, Illinois	1940
Decatur, Illinois	1938	Roswell, New Mexico	1946
Des Moines, Iowa	1939	Santa Fe, New Mexico	1946
Frankfort, Kentucky	1951	Schenectady, New York	1945
Freeport, Illinois	1952	Sioux Falls, South Dakota	1949
Glasgow, Kentucky	1949	Streator, Illinois	1950
Greenville, South Carolina	1950	St. Petersburg, Florida	1941
Hamilton, Ohio	1947	St. Louis, Missouri	1935
Jacksonville, Illinois	1950	Topeka, Kansas	1942
Jefferson City, Missouri	1952	Tuscola, Illinois	1952
Kansas City, Kansas	1938	Utica, New York	1948
Kankakee, Illinois	1945	West Palm Beach, Florida	1952
Lansing, Michigan	1937	Wichita, Kansas	1944
Lincoln, Nebraska	1951	Williamsburg, Virginia	1952
Marshall, Michigan	1950	Woodward, Oklahoma	1947
Mason City, Iowa	1940		

SATELLITE CITIES

Berkeley, Missouri	1941	Lincolnwood, Illinois	1945
Bettendorf, Iowa	1947	Maywood, Illinois	1950
Beverly Hills, California	1947	Morton Grove, Illinois	1945
Bloomfield, New Jersey	1948	New Westminster,	
Brentwood, Missouri	1952	British Columbia	1946
Clayton, Missouri	1941	Northfield, Illinois	1942
East Chicago, Indiana	1945	Oak Park, Illinois	1946
East Orange, New Jersey	1945	Olivette, Missouri	1940
East St. Louis, Illinois	1936	Richmond Heights,	
Edwardsville, Illinois	1945	Missouri	1941
Evanston, Illinois	1939	Skokie, Illinois	1945
Falls Church, Virginia	1950	University Park, Texas	1940
Ferguson, Missouri	1945	Webster Groves, Missouri	1937
Glendale, Ohio	1942	West Vancouver,	
Highland Park, Illinois	1946	British Columbia	1946
Irvington, New Jersey	1948	Wilmette, Illinois	1939
Kirkwood, Missouri	1941	Winnetka, Illinois	1940
LaGrange, Illinois	1939	Wyoming, Ohio	1946

URBAN AREAS

Battle Creek, Michigan	1947	Jefferson City, Missouri	1952
Brookhaven, Mississippi	1950	Lincoln, Nebraska	1951
Corpus Christi, Texas	1951	Sioux Falls, South Dakota	1949
Frankfort, Kentucky	1951	Streator, Illinois	1950
Freeport, Illinois	1952	Williamsburg, Virginia	1952
Jacksonville, Illinois	1950		

LAND USE CLASSIFICATION

Note: The following classifications are those used by the author's office.

MAIN CLASSES OF URBAN LAND USES

Use	Symbol	Use	Symbol
Single-family residences	R–1	Public and semipublic property	S.P.
Two-family dwellings	R–2	Light industry	L.I.
Multifamily dwellings	M	Heavy industry	H.I.
Commercial areas	C	Railroad property	R.R.
Parks and playgrounds	P		

ALPHABETICAL INDEX OF URBAN LAND USES AS CLASSIFIED IN ZONING SURVEYS

Abattoir	H.I.	Armory	S.P.
Academy, riding, dancing, etc.	C.	Arsenal, government property	S.P.
Acetylene gas manufacture	H.I.	Art gallery	S.P.
Acid manufacture	H.I.	Art shop	C.
Adding machine manufacture	L.I.	Artificial flower manufacture	L.I.
Agricultural implements manufacture	H.I.	Asbestos products manufacture	H.I.
Air products manufacture	H.I.	Asbestos products retail sale	C.
Airport	S.P.	Ash dumps	H.I.
Airplane repair and manufacture	H.I.	Asphalt manufacture, refining, or storage	H.I.
Aluminum manufacture	H.I.	Assaying	H.I.
Ammonia manufacture	H.I.	Assembly hall	S.P.
Ammunition manufacture	H.I.	Athletic field, private	C.
Amusement park	C.	Auditorium	S.P.
Aniline color or dye manufacture	H.I.	Automobile accessories, sale only	C.
Antique store	C.	Automobile assembly	L.I.
Apartment house (3 or more families)	M.	Automobile filling station	C.
		Automobile manufacturing	H.I.
Aquarium	S.P.	Automobile laundry	L.I.

Automobile rental agency	L.I.	Book shop	C.
Automobile repair	L.I.	Boot and shoe manufacture	L.I.
Automobile sales, only	C.	Botanical garden	S.P.
Aviation field	S.P.	Bottling works	L.I.
		Bowling alley	C.
Bag cleaning	H.I.	Box manufacture	H.I.
Bag manufacture	H.I.	Brass foundry	H.I.
Baggage transfer, storage,		Brewery	H.I.
warehouse	L.I.	Brick yard and kiln	H.I.
Bakery, retail	C	Broadcasting and	
Bakery, wholesale or em-		receiving station	C.
ploying 5 or more persons	L.I.	Bronze manufacture	H.I.
Bank	C.	Broom manufacture	L.I.
Bank equipment		Brush manufacture	H.I.
manufacture	H.I.	Building materials yard	L.I.
Barbecue stand	C.	Bus depot	C.
Barber shop	C.	Business equipment	
Barge terminal	L.I.	manufacture	H.I.
Barrel manufacture	H.I.		
Baseball park	C.	Cabinet maker	L.I.
Battery charging and repair	C.	Café	C.
Beer garden	C.	Cafeteria	C.
Beet sugar manufacture	H.I.	Calcimine manufacture	H.I.
Belting manufacture	H.I.	Camera shop	C.
Beverage, bottling only	L.I.	Can manufacture	H.I.
Beverage (malt and spirits)		Candle manufacture	H.I.
manufacture	H.I.	Candy manufacture	L.I.
Beverage (soft drink)		Candy store	C.
manufacture	L.I.	Canning and preserving	
Bicycle manufacture	H.I.	factory	L.I.
Bicycle repair	L.I.	Cap and hat manufacture	L.I.
Billiard parlor	C.	Car barns	L.I.
Blacksmith	L.I.	Car manufacture	H.I.
Blast furnace	H.I.	Car wheel foundry	H.I.
Bleachery	H.I.	Carborundum manufacture	H.I.
Bleaching powder		Carpenter shop	L.I.
manufacture	H.I.	Carpet cleaning	L.I.
Blooming mill	H.I.	Carriage and wagon	
Blueing manufacture	H.I.	manufacture	H.I.
Boarding house	M.	Casein manufacture	H.I.
Boat manufacture	H.I.	Cast iron pipe manufacture	H.I.
Boiler works	H.I.	Casting foundry	H.I.
Bolt and nut manufacture	H.I.	Caterer	C.
Book publishing	L.I.	Cattle shed	H.I.

Caustic soda manufacture	H.I.
Celluloid manufacture	H.I.
Chalk manufacture	H.I.
Charcoal manufacture and pulverizing	H.I.
Charitable institution	S.P.
Cheese manufacture	H.I.
Chemical manufacture	H.I.
Chemist shop	C.
Chicken hatchery	L.I.
Chlorine manufacture	H.I.
Chocolate and cocoa products	H.I.
Church	S.P.
Cider and vinegar manufacture	H.I.
Cigar manufacture	L.I.
Cigar store	C.
Cigarette manufacture	L.I.
City buildings	S.P.
Clay products	H.I.
Cleaning and pressing	L.I.
Clinic, public	S.P.
Clinic, private	C.
Clock factory	L.I.
Clothing manufacture	L.I.
Clothing store	C.
Clubs	S.P.
Coal mining	H.I.
Coal pocket	H.I.
Coal yard	L.I.
Coffee roasting	H.I.
Coffin manufacture	L.I.
Coke ovens	H.I.
Cold storage warehouse	L.I.
Coliseum	S.P.
College	S.P.
Comfort station	S.P.
Commission house	L.I.
Community house	S.P.
Concrete burial vault company	L.I.
Concrete batching or "ready mixed" plant	H.I.

Concrete products company	H.I.
Condensed milk manufacture	L.I.
Confectionery store	C.
Conservatory, commercial	C.
Contractors' storage yard	L.I.
Convent	S.P.
Convention building for private displays or rental	C.
Cooperage works	H.I.
Copper manufacture	H.I.
Cordage mill	H.I.
Correctional institution	S.P.
Corrugated metal manufacture	H.I.
Cosmetic manufacture	L.I.
Cotton ginning	H.I.
Cotton wadding manufacture	H.I.
Cotton yarn manufacture	H.I.
Cottonseed oil manufacture	H.I.
Court house	S.P.
Creamery, retail	C.
Creamery, wholesale	L.I.
Crematory	H.I.
Creosote treatment and manufacture	H.I.
Culvert pipe manufacture	H.I.
Dairy, retail	C.
Dairy, wholesale	L.I.
Dance hall	C.
Dancing school	C.
Delicatessen	C.
Dental laboratory	L.I.
Detention homes	S.P.
Distillation of coal, wood, bones	H.I.
Distillation of liquors, spirits, etc.	H.I.
Dog pound	S.P.
Dress shop	C.
Drive-in theater	C.
Drug manufacture	L.I.

Drug store	C.	Filling station	C.
Dry cleaning collection office	C.	Financial institution	C.
Dry cleaning establishment	L.I.	Fire brick manufacture	H.I.
Dry goods and notions store	C.	Fire clay products manufacture	H.I.
Dry goods, wholesale or storage	L.I.	Fire station	S.P.
Dumping station	H.I.	Fireworks manufacture or storage	H.I.
Dyeing and cleaning	L.I.	Fish curing	H.I.
Dyestuff manufacture	H.I.	Fish market	C.
		Fixture manufacture	H.I.
Electrical equipment, appliance and supply	C.	Flats (three or more families)	M.
Electrical power plant	L.I.	Florist shop	C.
Electrical repairing	L.I.	Flour and grain milling	H.I.
Electrical sign manufacture	L.I.	Flour and grain storage and elevators	L.I.
Electrical supply manufacture	H.I.	Food products, retail	C.
Eleemosynary institution	S.P.	Food products, manufacture	L.I.
Elevator manufacture	H.I.	Forge works	H.I.
Emery cloth manufacture	H.I.	Foundry	H.I.
Enameling and painting	L.I.	Fraternity house	M.
Engine manufacture	H.I.	Freight depot	R.R.
Engraving plant	L.I.	Frozen food locker	C.
Envelope manufacture	L.I.	Fruit and vegetable drying	L.I.
Excelsior manufacture	H.I.	Fruit and vegetable market	C.
Exhibition buildings	C.	Fuel distributing station	L.I.
Exhibition buildings, publicly owned	P.	Fuel gas manufacture	H.I.
Express office	C.	Fuel gas storage	L.I.
Express storage and delivery station	L.I.	Funeral parlor or chapel	C.
Exterminator or insect poison manufacture	H.I.	Fur and fur clothing store	C.
		Fur curing and tanning	H.I.
		Fur warehouse	L.I.
		Furnace manufacture	H.I.
Fat rendering	H.I.	Furniture factory	H.I.
Federal building	P.	Furniture and house furnishing store	C.
Feed manufacture	L.I.		
Feed store, retail	C.	Furniture warehouse or storage	L.I.
Feed, wholesale	L.I.		
Felt manufacture	H.I.	Garage, repair	L.I.
Ferry docks, passenger	S.P.	Garage, storage only	C.
Fertilizer manufacture	H.I.	Garment factory	L.I.

Gas (illuminating or heating) manufacture	H.I.	Hay, grain, and feed, retail,	C.
Gas (illuminating or heating) storage	L.I.	Hay, grain, and feed, wholesale	L.I.
Gasoline filling station	C.	Heating supplies and appliances manufacture	H.I.
Gasoline storage, wholesale	H.I.	Hide and tallow manufacture	H.I.
Gelatine manufacture	H.I.	Homes, religious, fraternal, eleemosynary	S.P.
Gift shop	C.	Horse, cat, and dog hospital	C.
Glass manufacture	H.I.	Horse-radish manufacture	H.I.
Glucose manufacture	H.I.	Horseshoeing	L.I.
Glue and fertilizer manufacture	H.I.	Hosiery mill	H.I.
Golf course	S.P.	Hosiery shop	C.
Golf driving range	C.	Hotel	C.
Golf course, miniature	C.	House of correction	S.P.
Government buildings	S.P.	Hydrochloric acid and derivatives manufacture	H.I.
Grain elevator	L.I.		
Graphite manufacture	H.I.		
Gravel pits	L.I.		
Grease and tallow manufacture	H.I.	Ice cream manufacture	L.I.
Greenhouse	C.	Ice cream store	C.
Grist mill	H.I.	Ice manufacture	L.I.
Grocery store, retail	C.	Ice skating rink	C.
Grocery store, wholesale	L.I.	Incinerator, public	S.P.
Gunpowder manufacture	H.I.	Incinerator, private	H.I.
Gutta percha manufacture	H.I.	Industrial school	S.P.
Gymnasium outfit manufacture	L.I.	Infirmary, city	P.
Gymnasium, private	C.	Infirmary, private	S.P.
Gymnasium, public	P.	Insane asylum	S.P.
Gypsum manufacture	H.I.	Insect poison manufacture	H.I.
		Institutes, religious, fraternal, eleemosynary	S.P.
Hair products factory	H.I.	Iron foundry	H.I.
Halls, public	S.P.	Iron (ornamental) works	H.I.
Halls, private	C.		
Hangars	S.P.	Japanning and shellacking works	H.I.
Hangars with repair facilities	L.I.	Jewelry store	C.
Hardware manufacture	H.I.	Jewelry manufacture	L.I.
Hardware store	C.	Junk yard	H.I.
Hat and cap store	C.	Jute manufacture	H.I.
Hat cleaning	L.I.	Kalsomine manufacture	H.I.
Hatchery	L.I.	Kennels	C.

Kerosene manufacture and storage	H.I.	Lubricating machinery manufacture	H.I.
Kindling manufacture	H.I.	Lubricating oil manufacture	H.I.
Knit goods manufacture	L.I.	Lumber mill	H.I.
		Lumber yard	L.I.
Laboratory	C.		
Lamp black manufacture	H.I.	Macaroni manufacture	L.I.
Lard manufacture	H.I.	Machine shop	H.I.
Lath manufacture	H.I.	Machinery manufacture	H.I.
Laundry	L.I.	Mail box manufacture	H.I.
Launderette (self-service)	C.	Malleable casting manufacture	H.I.
Laundry machinery manufacture	H.I.	Malt products manufacture	H.I.
Lead manufacture	H.I.	Marble quarry	H.I.
Lead (white) and all products manufacture	H.I.	Markets	C.
		Match manufacture	H.I.
Leather and leather goods manufacture	H.I.	Mattress manufacture	L.I.
		Meat and fish market	C.
Leather and leather goods shop	C.	Meat cutter and coffee grinder manufacture	H.I.
Leather, curing and tanning	H.I.	Meat packing plant	H.I.
Library	P.	Medicine (patent) manufacture	L.I.
Light and power manufacture	H.I.	Memorial home	S.P.
		Metal polish manufacture	H.I.
Light and power substation	L.I.	Metal products manufacture (except light products)	H.I.
Limb (artificial) manufacture	L.I.	Metal weather stripping manufacture	H.I.
Lime and cement warehouse	L.I.	Milk bottling plant	L.I.
Lime manufacture	H.I.	Milk depot, retail	C.
Linen goods manufacture	H.I.	Milk depot, wholesale	L.I.
Linoleum manufacture	H.I.	Millinery and artificial flower making	L.I.
Linseed oil manufacture	H.I.		
Livery and undertaking establishment	C.	Millinery and dress furnishing shop	C.
Livery stable	L.I.	Milling company	H.I.
Locomotive manufacture	H.I.	Mineral water distillation and bottling	L.I.
Lodge building	S.P.	Mission house	S.P.
Lodging house	M.	Molasses manufacture	H.I.
Loft building	L.I.	Monument works	H.I.
Loose-leaf book manufacture	L.I.	Mortuary	C.

Motorcycle manufacture	H.I.	Optical goods manufacture	L.I.
Motorcycle repair	L.I.	Optical goods store	C.
Motorcycle sale	C.	Ordnance manufacture	H.I.
Motordrome	C.	Ore dumps and elevators	H.I.
Moving company, office only	C.	Ore reduction	H.I.
		Organ manufacture	L.I.
Moving company, with storage facilities	L.I.	Orphan asylum	S.P.
		Outdoor theater	C.
Moving picture house	C.	Overall manufacture	L.I.
Museum	S.P.	Oxygen gas manufacture	H.I.
Music house	C.		
Musical instrument and sheet music shop	C.	Packing (meat, poultry) plant	H.I.
		Paint manufacture	H.I.
Nail manufacture	H.I.	Paint shop	L.I.
Natatorium, private	C.	Paint store	C.
Needle manufacture	H.I.	Paper or paper pulp manufacture	H.I.
Newsstand	C.		
Newspaper, office and printing	L.I.	Paper box manufacture	L.I.
		Paper can and tub manufacture	L.I.
Nitrating of cotton or other materials	H.I.	Paper products company	L.I.
		Paper sack manufacture	L.I.
Nitric acid or derivatives manufacture	H.I.	Parking lots, privately owned	C.
Notion shop	C.	Parking lots, publicly owned	P.
Nurseries, institutional or municipal	S.P.	Parks	P.
		Parochial school	S.P.
Nurses' home	S.P.	Pattern shop	H.I.
Nurseries, private	C.	Pawnbroker	C.
		Pencil factory	L.I.
Office building	C.	Penitentiary	P.
Office building on same site as industry (factory)	L.I.	Perfumery manufacture	L.I.
		Petroleum refining	H.I.
Office equipment and supply manufacture	L.I.	Petroleum storage, wholesale	H.I.
Office equipment and supply shop	C.	Petroleum wells	H.I.
		Pharmaceutical products manufacture	L.I.
Oil manufacture	H.I.		
Oil refinery	H.I.	Pharmacy	C.
Oil station	C.	Philanthropic uses	S.P.
Oilcloth manufacture	H.I.	Phonograph manufacture	L.I.
Old people's home	S.P.	Photo-engraving company	L.I.
Oleomargarine manufacture	H.I.	Photographer shop	C.
Opera house	C.		

Photographic supply and camera shop	C.	Radiator (heating) manufacture	H.I.
Piano manufacture	L.I.	Radio shop	C.
Piano store	C.	Radio manufacture	L.I.
Pickle manufacture	H.I.	Rag treatment or manufacture products from rags	H.I.
Picric acid or derivatives manufacture	H.I.	Railroad station	R.R.
Pin manufacture	H.I.	Railroad trackage and right of way	R.R.
Pipe (concrete) manufacture	H.I.		
Pipe (metal) manufacture	H.I.	Railroad yards	R.R.
Planing mill	H.I.	Raw hides and skins treatment and storage	H.I.
Plaster of Paris manufacture	H.I.		
Plating works	H.I.	Real estate office	C.
Playgrounds	P.	Reduction of ore, garbage, offal, etc.	H.I.
Plow manufacture	H.I.		
Plumbing supply manufacture	H.I.	Refreshment stand	C.
		Refrigerator manufacture	L.I.
Plumbing and heating fixture supply shop	C.	Refuse dump	H.I.
		Relay station	L.I.
Pole and shaft manufacture	H.I.	Relay station, department store	C.
Police station	S.P.		
Pool room	C.	Residence, 1-family	R–1
Poorhouse	S.P.	Residence, 2-family	R–2
Popcorn factory	L.I.	Residence, 3 or more families	M.
Post office	S.P.	Restaurant	C.
Potash manufacture	H.I.	Rice cleaning and polishing	H.I.
Poultry food manufacture	H.I.	Riding school	C.
Poultry slaughter	H.I.	Rivet manufacture	H.I.
Printing ink manufacture	H.I.	Rock crushing	H.I.
Printing press	L.I.	Roller skating rink	C.
Prison	S.P.	Rolling mill	H.I.
Produce store	C.	Rooming house	M.
Produce warehouse	L.I.	Rope manufacture	H.I.
Public buildings	P.	Roundhouse	R.R.
Public utilities plants	H.I. or L.I.	Row house	M.
Publishing company	L.I.	Rowing club	S.P.
Pumice manufacture	H.I.	Rubber cement manufacture	H.I.
Pump station	L.I.		
Pyroxylin manufacture	H.I.	Rubber manufacture	H.I.
		Rug cleaning	L.I.
Quarry, stone	H.I.	Rug manufacture	H.I.
Quilt manufacture	H.I.		
		Saddlery manufacture	L.I.
Race track, horse or dog	C.	Saloon	C.

Salt manufacture	H.I.	Soda water manufacture	L.I.
Salvage storage yard	H.I.	Soft drink stand	C.
Sand and gravel pits	L.I.	Soot blower manufacture	H.I.
Sand and gravel storage		Sorority house	M.
yard	L.I.	Soybean oil manufacture	H.I.
Sand paper manufacture	H.I.	Sporting goods manufacture	L.I.
Sanitorium	S.P.	Sporting goods store	C.
Sauerkraut manufacture	H.I.	Stable	L.I.
Sausage or sausage casing		Stadium, part of institution,	
manufacture	H.I.	school, etc.	S.P.
Sawdust manufacture	H.I.	Stadium, private	C.
Sawmill	H.I.	Stair manufacture	L.I.
Schools, public and private	S.P.	Stamping, metal	H.I.
Scrap iron, storage yard	H.I.	Starch manufacture	H.I.
Scrap metal reduction	H.I.	Stationery and supply store	C.
Screw and bolt manufacture	L.I.	Steamship agency	C.
Seed company	L.I.	Steel mill	H.I.
Sewer pipe manufacture	H.I.	Stock yards	H.I.
Sewage disposal plant		Stone crushing	H.I.
(municipal)	H.I. in S.P.	Stone cutting and screening	H.I.
Sheet metal shop	L.I.	Storage warehouse	L.I.
Shell grinding	H.I.	Stove and range	
Shellac manufacture	H.I.	manufacture	H.I.
Shingle manufacture	H.I.	Stove polish manufacture	H.I.
Shipyard	H.I.	Street railway yards and	
Shirt factory	L.I.	appurtenances	L.I.
Shoe blacking manufacture	H.I.	Structural iron and steel	
Shoe manufacture	H.I.	manufacture	H.I.
Shoe repair shop	C.	Substation electric power	
Shoe store, retail	C.	and light company	L.I.
Shovel manufacture	H.I.	Sugar refining	H.I.
Sign painting	L.I.	Sulphur, sulphuric acid, or	
Silk manufacture	L.I.	derivatives manufacture	H.I.
Size manufacture	H.I.	Sweeping compound	
Skating rink	C.	manufacture	H.I.
Slag pile	H.I.	Swimming pool, public	P.
Slate quarry	H.I.	Swimming pool, commercial	C.
Smelting metals	H.I.	Synagogue	S.P.
Snuff manufacture	H.I.	Syrup and preserve	
Soap manufacture	H.I.	manufacture	H.I.
Soda and washing com-			
pound manufacture	H.I.	Tack manufacture	H.I.
Soda ash manufacture	H.I.	Tailor shop	L.I.
Soda fountain	C.	Tallow manufacture	H.I.

Tanning and curing of hides	H.I.	Trunk manufacture	L.I.
Tar distillation or manufacture	H.I.	Turpentine manufacture	H.I.
Tar paper manufacture	H.I.	Two-family dwelling	R-2
Tar products manufacture	H.I.		
Taxicab storage, repair	L.I.	Undertaking establishment	C.
Tea and spice packing	L.I.	U. S. Government building	P.
Tea and spice retail	C.	Upholstery manufacture	L.I.
Telegraph office	C.	Upholstery shop	C.
Telephone exchange	L.I.		
Telephone substation	L.I.	Variety store	C.
Television aerials (classed with building to which attached)	L.I.	Varnish manufacture	H.I.
		Vegetable market	C.
		Vinegar manufacture	H.I.
Television manufacture	L.I.	Vocational school	S.P.
Television stations	C.	Vulcanizing shop (rubber)	L.I.
Television repair	C.		
Television sending or relay towers	L.I.	Wagon manufacture	H.I.
		Wagon shop	L.I.
Television stores	C.	Wall paper manufacture	L.I.
Tenements	M.	Warehouse	L.I.
Terra cotta manufacture	H.I.	Washing machine manufacture	L.I.
Textile machinery	H.I.		
Textile manufacture	L.I.	Washing powder manufacture	H.I.
Theater	C.		
Thermometer or thermostat manufacture	L.I.	Washing soda manufacture	H.I.
		Waste paper products manufacture	H.I.
Tile manufacture	H.I.		
Tin foil manufacture	H.I.	Watch manufacture	L.I.
Tin products, wholesale	L.I.	Water company appurtenances	L.I.
Tin products, manufacture	H.I.		
Tin refining	H.I.	Water company property	S.P.
Tinsmith shop	L.I.	Waterproofing treatment and manufacture	L.I.
Tire manufacture	H.I.		
Tire repair shop	L.I.	Welding shop	L.I.
Tobacco manufacture	H.I.	Wharf	L.I.
Tobacco shop	C.	White lead manufacture	H.I.
Tool manufacture	H.I.	Wholesale produce storage or market	L.I.
Tourist camp	C.		
Trailer camp	C.	Window shade manufacture	L.I.
Transfer company, baggage, storage	L.I.	Wire brush manufacture	L.I.
		Wire manufacture	H.I.
		Wood preserving treatment	H.I.
Trunk and leather goods shop	C.	Wood products manufacture	L.I.

Wood pulp manufacture	H.I.	Yeast manufacture	H.I.
Woodworking shops, small	L.I.	Y.M.C.A.	S.P.
Wool scouring or pulling	H.I.	Y.W.C.A.	S.P.
Woven goods manufacture	L.I.		
Worsted goods manufacture	L.I.	Zinc products manufacture	H.I.
Wrecking material yard	H.I.	Zinc refining	H.I.

APPENDIX C

METHOD

The summary tables presented in the text for developed area, total area, and area per 100 population by use are arithmetic means of the land area and population of all cities in each population group. Thus the sum of the area for all cities in the class interval has been divided by the total population (in 100's) of cities in the group to obtain the ratio for the group.

Inspection of the original data presented in Tables 1, 2, 5, 6, 9, and 10 will reveal that this method emphasizes the influence of the larger cities in each class interval in each of the four categories of cities. The effect is particularly noticeable where class intervals are wide, as in the 50,000 and less population class for central cities.

As a consequence of the method, the data presented in the total columns of Tables 3, 4, 7, 8, and 11 should be used with considerable caution. It will be noted that similar totals are not presented in the smaller tables in the text, and that the text emphasizes the wide range of conditions observed even in cities of the same class interval.

Urban Land Uses (1932) sought to overcome some of these difficulties by presenting weighted averages. It will be noted that the 1932 book was based upon such a limited number of cities that grouping by population class presented serious problems. For this reason, the summary tables in that work were computed by dividing the sum of the ratios for all cities in the class interval by the number of cities in the group.

The much larger number of cities utilized in the present study makes it possible to present data by city size. For this reason, the data have been presented and summarized by class interval, and appear for all cities in each category only in the tables identified above.

Tables 13 and 14 which follow show the 1932 results and the 1953 results computed on both bases. These tables emphasize the variations resulting from choice of method. They are presented for the use of research workers and should not be utilized for other purposes.

Finally, it should be noted that the two comparative tables do not indicate trends in land use. The differences observed result from differences in the number of cities, the character of the cities covered by the study, and from the method of computing means.

TABLES

TABLE 1. LAND USE IN 53 CENTRAL CITIES. Percentage of total developed area and total city area occupied by major urban uses.

City And Population Group	Year Of Survey	Population At Date Of Survey [a]	Single-Family Dwellings			Two-Family Dwellings			Multi-Family Dwellings			Commercial Use		
			Area In Acres	% Of Total Developed Area	% Of Total City Area	Area In Acres	% Of Total Developed Area	% Of Total City Area	Area In Acres	% Of Total Developed Area	% Of Total City Area	Area In Acres	% Of Total Developed Area	% of Total City Area
50,000 or less														
1 Atchison, Kansas	1941	12,648	556.59	38.92	30.44	3.99	0.28	0.22	6.54	0.46	0.36	41.10	2.87	2.25
2 Bar Harbor, Maine	1947	3,300	154.50	55.84	46.76	4.90[b]	1.77	1.48	-	-	-	17.10	6.18	5.18
3 Baton Rouge, Louisiana	1946	34,719	766.53	33.33	22.60	57.86	2.51	1.71	34.27	1.49	1.01	82.20	3.57	2.42
4 Battle Creek, Michigan	1947	43,453	1,323.00	33.73	19.30	223.50	5.70	3.26	112.30	2.86	1.64	130.70	3.33	1.91
5 Brookhaven, Mississippi	1950	8,220	404.90	44.06	29.27	31.60	3.44	2.29	22.60	2.46	1.63	26.00	2.83	1.88
6 Carlsbad, New Mexico	1945	7,116	343.30	33.97	22.25	19.10	1.89	1.24	9.50	0.94	0.61	37.00	3.66	2.40
7 Centralia, Illinois	1940	17,000	558.60	43.28	31.47	6.50	0.50	0.37	6.40	0.50	0.36	39.90	3.09	2.25
8 Frankfort, Kentucky	1951	11,916	237.50	27.03	18.61	70.30	8.00	5.51	39.30	4.47	3.08	30.70	3.50	2.41
9 Freeport, Illinois	1952	22,467	782.90	41.28	29.32	101.90	5.37	3.82	31.60	1.67	1.18	46.90	2.47	1.76
10 Glasgow, Kentucky	1949	7,040	423.70	51.14	29.59	53.00	6.04	3.70	20.80	2.51	1.45	30.30	3.66	2.12
11 Jacksonville, Illinois	1950	20,600	930.30	43.23	29.81	90.90	4.22	2.91	66.30	3.08	2.13	49.50	2.30	1.59
12 Jefferson City, Missouri	1952	23,200	779.90	30.24	12.81	103.40	4.01	1.70	47.50	1.84	0.78	92.50	3.59	1.52
13 Kankakee, Illinois	1945	22,241	678.40	33.33	26.50	133.10	6.54	5.20	15.40	0.76	0.60	58.90	2.89	2.30
14 Marshall, Michigan	1950	5,740	399.20	35.67	17.18	39.06	3.49	1.68	9.71	0.87	0.42	28.97	2.59	1.25
15 Mason City, Iowa	1940	25,500	866.30	28.77	10.83	50.70	1.68	0.63	23.60	0.78	0.30	56.90	1.89	0.71
16 Mexico, Missouri	1952	12,500	480.40	25.46	11.21	51.70	2.74	1.21	17.80	0.94	0.41	41.30	2.19	0.96
17 Muskogee, Oklahoma	1945	37,500	1,424.49	35.53	24.58	72.94	1.82	1.26	25.19	0.63	0.43	107.92	2.69	1.86
18 Naples, Florida	1952	1,740	216.20	26.19	3.31	12.70	1.54	0.19	14.10	1.71	0.22	52.00	6.30	0.79
19 Petersburg, Virginia	1943	30,631	669.31	26.41	18.55	155.92	6.15	4.32	35.08	1.38	0.97	49.29	1.95	1.37
20 Quincy, Illinois	1945	42,750	1,275.00	38.66	33.60	245.70	7.45	6.47	76.80	2.33	2.02	87.20	2.64	2.30
21 Rock Island, Illinois	1940	42,000	1,186.50	37.87	22.39	160.90	5.14	3.04	45.10	1.44	0.85	91.90	2.93	1.73
22 Roswell, New Mexico	1946	20,400	847.07	27.90	19.74	27.14	0.89	0.63	17.05	0.56	0.40	69.37	2.29	1.61
23 Santa Fe, New Mexico	1946	24,320	776.72	35.80	4.69	19.61	0.90	0.12	19.23	0.89	0.12	56.98	2.63	0.35
24 Streator, Illinois	1950	17,268	830.20	45.82	37.87	38.20	2.11	1.74	10.40	0.57	0.48	45.90	2.53	2.09
25 Tuscola, Illinois	1952	2,967	204.50	39.63	32.93	11.50	2.23	1.85	2.78	0.54	0.45	21.50	4.17	3.46
26 West Palm Beach, Florida	1952	44,000	1,165.00	28.44	12.92	254.50	6.21	2.82	194.90	4.76	2.16	266.00	6.49	2.95
27 Williamsburg, Virginia	1952	3,500	170.70	15.10	9.33	13.50	1.19	0.74	45.30	4.01	2.47	51.30	4.54	2.80

[a]Estimated, or interpolated from U.S. Census. [b]Includes multifamily dwelling areas. [c]Includes parks and playgrounds. [d]Includes heavy industry. [e]Includes railroad property.

City And Population Group	Industry Area in Acres	Industry % of Total Developed Area	Industry % of Total City Area	Heavy Industry Area in Acres	Heavy Industry % of Total Developed Area	Heavy Industry % of Total City Area	Property Area in Acres	Property % of Total Developed Area	Property % of Total City Area	Playgrounds Area in Acres	Playgrounds % of Total Developed Area	Playgrounds % of Total City Area
50,000 or less												
1 Atchison, Kansas	33.69	2.36	1.84	13.95	0.98	0.76	61.42	4.29	3.36	134.19	9.38	7.34
2 Bar Harbor, Maine	12.40	4.48	3.75	0.00	0.00	0.00	0.00	0.00	0.00	-	-	-
3 Baton Rouge, Louisiana	75.82	3.30	2.23	5.84	0.25	0.17	235.40	10.23	6.94	114.65	4.98	3.38
4 Battle Creek, Michigan	154.30	3.93	2.25	151.00	3.85	2.20	159.60	4.07	2.33	288.90	7.37	4.21
5 Brookhaven, Mississippi	45.80	4.99	3.31	33.80	3.68	2.44	51.70	5.63	3.74	12.50	1.36	0.90
6 Carlsbad, New Mexico	35.60	3.52	2.31	7.60	0.75	0.49	78.10	7.73	5.06	47.10	4.66	3.05
7 Centralia, Illinois	4.50	0.35	0.25	43.10	3.34	2.43	99.80	7.73	5.62	3.20	0.25	0.18
8 Frankfort, Kentucky	23.40	2.66	1.83	14.40	1.64	1.13	31.00	3.53	2.43	3.70	0.42	0.29
9 Freeport, Illinois	53.40	2.82	2.00	45.80	2.41	1.71	132.90	7.01	4.98	40.80	2.15	1.53
10 Glasgow, Kentucky	40.50	4.89	2.83	9.40	1.13	0.66	7.70	0.93	0.54	1.40	0.17	0.10
11 Jacksonville, Illinois	36.10	1.68	1.16	32.20	1.50	1.03	78.40	3.64	2.51	10.70	0.50	0.34
12 Jefferson City, Missouri	51.40	1.99	0.84	26.50	1.03	0.44	98.00	3.80	1.61	253.40	9.83	4.16
13 Kankakee, Illinois	33.30	1.64	1.30	58.90	2.89	2.30	115.20	5.66	4.50	89.60	4.40	3.50
14 Marshall, Michigan	32.63	2.91	1.40	58.25	5.20	2.51	29.45	2.63	1.27	8.01	0.72	0.34
15 Mason City, Iowa	85.40	2.84	1.07	382.20	12.69	4.78	358.10	11.89	4.48	41.40	1.37	0.52
16 Mexico, Missouri	31.60	1.67	0.74	159.00	8.42	3.71	91.60	4.85	2.14	101.00	5.35	2.36
17 Muskogee, Oklahoma	48.24	1.20	0.83	13.66	0.34	0.24	213.61	5.33	3.69	192.98	4.81	3.33
18 Naples, Florida	6.30	0.76	0.10	8.10	0.98	0.12	57.60	6.98	0.88	10.70	1.30	0.16
19 Petersburg, Virginia	183.98	7.26	5.10	37.59	1.48	1.04	73.86	2.92	2.05	528.75	20.87	14.66
20 Quincy, Illinois	127.10	3.86	3.35	87.30	2.65	2.30	62.30	1.89	1.64	182.50	5.53	4.81
21 Rock Island, Illinois	115.90	3.70	2.19	105.30	3.36	1.99	143.40	4.58	2.71	120.80	3.86	2.28
22 Roswell, New Mexico	74.16	2.44	1.73	111.48	3.67	2.60	39.14	1.29	0.91	53.90	1.78	1.25
23 Santa Fe, New Mexico	53.24	2.45	0.32	0.00	0.00	0.00	22.63	1.04	0.14	64.46	2.97	0.39
24 Streator, Illinois	32.10	1.77	1.47	103.70	5.72	4.73	143.90	7.94	6.57	25.30	1.40	1.15
25 Tuscola, Illinois	14.22[d]	2.76	2.29	-	-	-	18.50	3.59	2.98	25.00	4.84	4.03
26 West Palm Beach, Florida	87.50	2.14	0.97	51.10	1.25	0.57	250.20	6.11	2.77	410.30	10.01	4.55
27 Williamsburg, Virginia	17.20	1.52	0.94	8.20	0.73	0.45	20.60	1.82	1.13	2.90	0.26	0.16
28 Woodward, Oklahoma	16.55	1.98	1.51	6.03	0.72	0.55	67.60	8.08	6.17	21.32	2.55	1.95

City And Population Group	Public And Semi-Public Property			Streets			Vacant Areas		Water Areas		Total Developed Area	Total City Area	
	Area in Acres	% of Total Developed Areas	% of Total City Area	Area in Acres	% of Total Developed Area	% of Total City Area	Area in Acres	% of Total City Area	Area in Acres	% of Total City Area	Area in Acres	Area in Acres	
50,000 or less													
1 Atchison, Kansas	69.47	4.86	3.80	509.12	35.60	27.84	398.42	21.79	0.00	0.00	1,430.06	1,828.48	1
2 Bar Harbor, Maine	44.00 c	15.90	13.32	43.80	15.83	13.26	53.70	16.25	0.00	0.00	276.70	330.40	2
3 Baton Rouge, Louisiana	265.61	11.54	7.83	662.49	28.80	19.53	884.43	26.07	207.16	6.11	2,300.67	3,392.26	3
4 Battle Creek, Michigan	339.40	8.65	4.95	1,040.00	26.51	15.17	2,690.20	39.24	243.10	3.54	3,922.70	6,856.00	4
5 Brookhaven, Mississippi	67.10	7.30	4.85	222.80	24.25	16.11	464.50	33.58	0.00	0.00	918.80	1,383.30	5
6 Carlsbad, New Mexico	56.00	5.54	3.63	377.30	37.34	24.45	532.50	34.51	0.00	0.00	1,010.60	1,543.10	6
7 Centralia, Illinois	26.00	2.01	1.46	502.60	38.95	28.32	484.40	27.29	0.00	0.00	1,290.60	1,775.00	7
8 Frankfort, Kentucky	215.80	24.56	16.91	212.50	24.19	16.65	346.80	27.17	50.80	3.98	878.60	1,276.20	8
9 Freeport, Illinois	146.70	7.73	5.49	513.90	27.09	19.24	682.80	25.57	90.70	3.40	1,896.80	2,670.30	9
10 Glasgow, Kentucky	94.70	11.43	6.61	147.00	17.74	10.26	603.50	42.14	0.00	0.00	828.50	1,432.00	10
11 Jacksonville, Illinois	387.00	17.99	12.40	470.50	21.86	15.08	943.60	30.24	25.00	0.80	2,151.90	3,120.50	11
12 Jefferson City, Missouri	462.90	17.95	7.60	663.40	25.72	10.89	3,510.10	57.65	0.00	0.00	2,578.90	6,089.00	12
13 Kankakee, Illinois	81.90	4.03	3.20	770.60	37.86	30.10	455.70	17.80	69.00	2.70	2,035.30	2,560.00	13
14 Marshall, Michigan	245.61	21.94	10.57	268.38	23.98	11.55	1,145.21	49.28	59.32	2.55	1,119.27	2,323.80	14
15 Mason City, Iowa	267.10	8.87	3.34	880.10	29.22	11.01	4,885.20	61.10	98.40	1.23	3,011.80	7,995.40	15
16 Mexico, Missouri	490.20	25.98	11.43	422.70	22.40	9.86	2,399.60	55.97	0.00	0.00	1,887.30	4,286.90	16
17 Muskogee, Oklahoma	549.32	13.70	9.48	1,361.01	33.95	23.48	1,785.89	30.82	0.00	0.00	4,009.36	5,795.25	17
18 Naples, Florida	165.00	19.98	2.52	282.90	34.26	4.33	4,594.40	70.25	1,120.00	17.13	825.60	6,540.00	18
19 Petersburg, Virginia	273.36	10.79	7.58	526.78	20.79	14.60	936.15	25.95	137.60	3.81	2,533.92	3,607.67	19
20 Quincy, Illinois	167.30	5.07	4.41	986.60	29.92	26.00	497.20	13.10	0.00	0.00	3,297.80	3,795.00	20
21 Rock Island, Illinois	283.40	9.05	5.35	879.30	28.07	16.60	2,165.30	40.87	0.00	0.00	3,132.50	5,297.80	21
22 Roswell, New Mexico	960.09	31.63	22.37	836.36	27.55	19.49	1,256.13	29.27	0.00	0.00	3,035.76	4,291.89	22
23 Santa Fe, New Mexico	604.80	27.87	3.65	552.19	25.45	3.33	14,381.44	86.89	0.00	0.00	2,169.86	16,551.30	23
24 Streator, Illinois	46.50	2.57	2.12	535.80	29.57	24.44	357.50	16.31	22.50	1.03	1,812.00	2,192.00	24
25 Tuscola, Illinois	52.00	10.07	8.37	166.00	32.17	26.73	105.00	16.91	0.00	0.00	516.00	621.00	25
26 West Palm Beach, Florida	274.00	6.69	3.04	1,143.20	27.90	12.68	3,969.80	44.02	952.00	10.55	4,096.70	9,018.50	26
27 Williamsburg, Virginia													27

City and Population Group	Year Of Survey	Population At Date Of Survey	Area In Acres	% Of Total Developed Area	% Of Total City Area	Area In Acres	% Of Total Developed Area	% Of Total City Area	Area In Acres	% Of Total Developed Area	% Of Total City Area	Area In Acres	% Of Total Developed Area	% Of Total City Area
50,000 – 100,000														
29 Binghampton, New York	1948	85,397	1,129.00	25.35	16.32	552.90	12.42	7.99	171.70	3.86	2.48	162.30	3.64	2.35
30 Davenport, Iowa	1945	75,000	2,491.00	38.31	19.29	132.00	2.03	1.02	85.00	1.31	0.66	116.00	1.79	0.90
31 Decatur, Illinois	1938	57,500	1,909.50	45.12	36.77	64.60	1.53	1.24	30.60	0.72	0.59	124.30	2.94	2.39
32 Greenville, South Carolina	1950	57,932	2,262.20	40.87	22.63	252.00	4.55	2.52	276.60	5.00	2.77	205.00	3.70	2.05
33 Hamilton, Ohio	1947	54,500	1,382.00	36.93	30.72	146.30	3.91	3.25	52.80	1.41	1.17	95.10	2.54	2.11
34 Lansing, Michigan	1937	83,500	1,962.40	35.26	25.62	116.10	2.09	1.51	36.10	0.65	0.47	131.20	2.36	1.71
35 Lincoln, Nebraska	1951	97,423	3,084.00	30.22	21.22	123.00	1.21	0.85	142.00	1.39	0.98	182.00	1.78	1.25
36 Portsmouth, Virginia	1946	81,957	653.00	22.02	15.67	319.20	10.77	7.66	118.90	4.01	2.85	81.00	2.73	1.94
37 Racine, Wisconsin	1938	72,000	1,114.00	28.46	19.55	311.70	7.96	5.47	40.30	1.03	0.71	163.40	4.17	2.87
38 St. Petersburg, Florida	1941	60,812	2,368.80	21.67	7.07	155.40	1.42	0.46	272.90	2.50	0.81	185.70	1.70	0.55
39 Sioux Falls, South Dakota	1949	51,000	1,357.10	23.42	17.11	105.80	1.83	1.33	116.50	2.01	1.47	148.80	2.57	1.88
40 Schenectady, New York	1945	87,549	1,055.30	20.76	15.89	650.30	12.79	9.79	164.30	3.23	2.47	205.60	4.04	3.10
41 Topeka, Kansas	1942	67,802	2,334.50	40.23	31.26	144.80	2.50	1.94	87.70	1.51	1.17	127.50	2.20	1.71
100,000 – 250,000														
42 Corpus Christi, Texas	1951	110,900	3,603.20	39.09	4.44	182.60	1.98	0.22	249.20	2.70	0.31	458.90	4.98	0.57
43 Des Moines, Iowa	1939	153,000	7,035.10	39.53	19.80	111.60	0.63	0.31	377.10	2.12	1.06	415.90	2.34	1.17
44 Kansas City, Kansas	1938	125,000	3,257.50	36.83	25.04	157.40	1.78	1.21	66.60	0.75	0.51	216.70	2.45	1.67
45 Oklahoma City, Oklahoma	1945	226,000	5,484.84	39.63	32.55	640.71	4.63	3.80	267.01	1.93	1.58	350.24	2.53	2.08
46 Richmond, Virginia	1942	193,042	4,487.80	29.94	17.65	604.00	4.03	2.37	337.60	2.25	1.33	412.40	2.75	1.62
47 Utica, New York	1948	106,750	1,072.60	16.25	10.33	667.00	10.11	6.42	279.00	4.23	2.68	278.00	4.21	2.68
48 Wichita, Kansas	1944	114,966	4,483.40	39.53	31.30	591.50	5.21	4.13	249.80	2.20	1.74	261.70	2.31	1.83
250,000 and Over														
49 Dallas, Texas	1944	338,000	9,305.00	35.63	28.93	2,143.75	8.21	6.66	813.40	3.12	2.53	608.33	2.33	1.89
50 Dayton, Ohio	1952	255,474	5,446.00	37.78	31.41	768.00	5.33	4.43	443.00	3.07	2.55	811.00	5.63	4.68
51 Memphis, Tennessee	1939	260,000	7,432.20	37.49	23.87	865.10	4.36	2.78	498.30	2.51	1.60	582.40	2.94	1.87
52 Newark, New Jersey	1945	429,760	1,044.50	8.44	6.36	825.00	6.66	5.02	1,033.00	8.34	6.28	791.00	6.39	4.81
53 St. Louis, Missouri	1935	821,960	6,817.00	20.39	17.11	2,581.90	7.72	6.48	2,424.50	7.25	6.09	1,735.30	5.19	4.36

a Estimated, or interpolated from U.S. Census. b Includes multifamily dwelling areas. c Includes parks and playgrounds. d Includes heavy industry. e Includes railroad property

TABLE 1 (continued). LAND USE IN 53 CENTRAL CITIES. Percentage of total developed area and total city area occupied by major urban uses.

City And Population Group	Light Industry			Heavy Industry			Railroad Property			Parks And Playgrounds		
	Area in Acres	% of Total Developed Area	% of Total City Area	Area in Acres	% of Total Developed Area	% of Total City Area	Area in Acres	% of Total Developed Area	% of Total City Area	Area in Acres	% of Total Developed Area	% of Total City Area
50,000 – 100,000												
29 Binghampton, New York	227.60	5.11	3.29	61.10	1.37	0.88	234.10	5.26	3.38	469.80	10.55	6.79
30 Davenport, Iowa	104.00	1.60	0.81	114.00	1.75	0.88	254.00	3.91	1.97	794.00	12.21	6.15
31 Decatur, Illinois	57.50	1.36	1.11	202.40	4.78	3.90	240.30	5.68	4.63	285.20	6.74	5.49
32 Greenville, South Carolina	127.60	2.30	1.28	60.60	1.09	0.61	160.10	2.89	1.60	150.50	2.72	1.50
33 Hamilton, Ohio	110.80	2.96	2.46	203.00	5.43	4.51	150.00	4.01	3.34	315.00	8.42	7.00
34 Lansing, Michigan	198.10	3.56	2.59	344.80	6.19	4.50	192.90	3.47	2.52	535.20	9.62	6.99
35 Lincoln, Nebraska	156.00	1.53	1.07	52.00	0.51	0.36	716.00	7.02	4.92	385.00	3.77	2.65
36 Portsmouth, Virginia	79.60	2.69	1.91	71.90	2.42	1.72	479.30	16.16	11.50	17.50	0.59	0.42
37 Racine, Wisconsin	69.50	1.77	1.22	228.80°	5.84	4.02	—	—	—	444.50	11.35	7.80
38 St. Petersburg, Florida	65.30	0.59	0.19	43.40	0.39	0.13	251.00	2.30	0.75	372.20	3.40	1.11
39 Sioux Falls, South Dakota	127.30	2.20	1.61	142.40	2.46	1.80	336.00	5.80	4.24	499.80	8.63	6.30
40 Schenectady, New York	130.60	2.57	1.97	423.50	8.33	6.37	217.90	4.29	3.28	427.20	8.40	6.43
41 Topeka, Kansas	110.00	1.90	1.47	68.00	1.17	0.91	394.50	6.79	5.28	181.40	3.13	2.43
100,000 – 250,000												
42 Corpus Christi, Texas	282.60	3.07	0.35	410.30	4.45	0.51	149.60	1.62	0.18	197.70	2.14	0.24
43 Des Moines, Iowa	228.90	1.29	0.64	418.20	2.35	1.18	948.80	5.33	2.67	1,003.70	5.64	2.83
44 Kansas City, Kansas	132.90	1.50	1.02	632.90	7.16	4.87	1,128.30	12.76	8.67	309.50	3.50	2.38
45 Oklahoma City, Oklahoma	285.36	2.06	1.69	354.23	2.56	2.10	516.84	3.73	3.07	878.13	6.35	5.21
46 Richmond, Virginia	648.50	4.33	2.55	501.20	3.34	1.97	738.70	4.93	2.90	1,029.20	6.87	4.05
47 Utica, New York	171.00	2.59	1.65	374.00	5.67	3.60	622.50	9.43	5.99	665.70	10.09	6.41
48 Wichita, Kansas	203.90	1.80	1.42	182.10	1.61	1.27	353.10	3.11	2.46	608.40	5.36	4.25
250,000 and Over												
49 Dallas, Texas	382.61	1.47	1.19	413.66	1.58	1.29	722.06	2.76	2.24	4,020.37	15.40	12.50
50 Dayton, Ohio	948.00	6.58	5.47	133.00	0.92	0.77	334.00	2.32	1.93	478.00	3.31	2.76
51 Memphis, Tennessee	922.90	4.66	2.96	987.00	4.98	3.17	1,098.50	5.54	3.53	1,128.80	5.70	3.63

#	City And Population Group	Area in Acres	% of Total Developed Areas	% of Total City Area	Area in Acres	% of Total Developed Area	% of Total City Area	Area in Acres	% of Total City Area	Area in Acres	% of City Area	Area in Acres	Area in Acres	#
	50,000 - 100,000													
29	Binghampton, New York	593.00	13.32	8.57	851.70	19.12	12.31	2,055.50	29.71	410.30	5.93	4,453.20	6,919.00	29
30	Davenport, Iowa	722.00	11.10	5.59	1,690.00	25.99	13.09	5,533.00	42.86	876.00	6.78	6,502.00	12,911.00	30
31	Decatur, Illinois	195.00	4.61	3.76	1,122.50	26.52	21.62	960.90	18.50	0.00	0.00	4,231.90	5,192.80	31
32	Greenville, South Carolina	746.30	13.48	7.47	1,295.10	23.40	12.96	4,416.10	44.19	41.90	0.42	5,536.00	9,994.00	32
33	Hamilton, Ohio	308.20	8.24	6.85	978.40	26.15	21.75	525.00	11.67	232.50	5.17	3,741.60	4,499.10	33
34	Lansing, Michigan	465.30	8.36	6.07	1,582.90	28.44	20.67	1,899.30	24.80	195.20	2.55	5,565.00	7,659.50	34
35	Lincoln, Nebraska	1,064.00	10.42	7.32	4,301.00	42.15	29.59	4,330.00	29.79	0.00	0.00	10,205.00	14,535.00	35
36	Portsmouth, Virginia	324.20	10.93	7.78	820.70	27.68	19.69	809.30	19.41	393.80	9.45	2,965.20	4,168.30	36
37	Racine, Wisconsin	293.10	7.48	5.14	1,250.60	31.94	21.95	1,714.80	30.10	66.80	1.17	3,915.90	5,697.50	37
38	St. Petersburg, Florida	950.50	8.70	2.84	6,267.50	57.33	18.70	22,171.20	66.14	418.30	1.25	10,932.70	33,522.20	38
39	Sioux Falls, South Dakota	1,371.50	23.67	17.29	1,588.10	27.41	20.02	2,011.60	25.36	126.10	1.59	5,793.30	7,931.00	39
40	Schenectady, New York	739.00	14.53	11.12	1,070.90	21.06	16.12	1,471.10	22.14	87.60	1.32	5,084.60	6,643.30	40
41	Topeka, Kansas	313.60	5.40	4.20	2,041.00	35.17	27.33	1,438.00	19.26	227.00	3.04	5,803.00	7,468.00	41
	100,000 - 250,000													
42	Corpus Christi, Texas	1,050.10	11.39	1.29	2,634.20	28.58	3.24	4,753.80	5.86	67,218.80	82.79	9,218.40	81,191.00	42
43	Des Moines, Iowa	2,807.30	15.77	7.90	4,450.10	25.00	12.52	17,049.30	47.99	684.50	1.93	17,796.70	35,530.50	43
44	Kansas City, Kansas	430.20	4.86	3.31	2,512.70	28.41	19.32	3,422.60	26.31	740.40	5.69	8,844.70	13,007.70	44
45	Oklahoma City, Oklahoma	780.01	5.64	4.63	4,281.61	30.94	25.41	2,913.20	17.29	100.00	0.59	13,838.98	16,852.18	45
46	Richmond, Virginia	2,064.70	13.77	8.12	4,165.00	27.79	16.38	8,675.10	34.11	1,766.50	6.95	14,989.10	25,430.70	46
47	Utica, New York	1,171.20	17.75	11.27	1,298.30	19.67	12.50	3,511.70	33.81	276.00	2.66	6,599.30	10,387.00	47
48	Wichita, Kansas	971.90	8.57	6.78	3,432.50	30.30	24.00	2,654.20	18.53	328.50	2.29	11,343.30	14,326.00	48
	250,000 and Over													
49	Dallas, Texas	1,424.70	5.46	4.43	6,276.96	24.04	19.52	5,865.44	18.24	186.33	0.58	26,110.84	32,162.61	49
50	Dayton, Ohio	1,403.00	9.73	8.09	3,651.00	25.33	21.06	2,648.00	15.27	274.00	1.58	14,415.00	17,337.00	50
51	Memphis, Tennessee	1,656.10	8.35	5.32	4,652.90	23.47	14.95	10,253.20	32.93	1,056.00	3.39	19,824.20	31,133.40	51
52	Newark, New Jersey	2,209.00	17.84	13.44	2,858.80	23.09	17.39	2,723.20	16.57	1,331.20	8.10	12,380.80	16,435.20	52
53	St. Louis, Missouri	3,485.50	10.42	8.75	8,836.00	26.42	22.18	6,395.10	16.05	0.00	0.00	33,440.90	39,836.00	53

a Estimated, or interpolated from U.S. Census. b Includes multifamily dwelling areas. c Includes parks and playgrounds. d Includes heavy industry. e Includes railroad property

TABLE 2. LAND USE IN 53 CENTRAL CITIES. Acres per 100 persons occupied by major urban uses.

	City and Population Group	Year of Survey	Population At Date of Survey [a]	Single-Family Dwellings		Two-Family Dwellings		Multi-Family Dwellings		Commercial Use		Light Industry	
				Area in Acres	Acres Per 100 Persons	Area in Acres	Acres Per 100 Persons	Area in Acres	Acres Per 100 Persons	Area in Acres	Acres Per 100 Persons	Area in Acres	Acres Per 100 Persons
	50,000 or Less												
1	Atchinson, Kansas	1941	12,648	556.59	4.40	3.99	0.03	6.54	0.05	41.10	0.32	33.69	0.27
2	Bar Harbor, Maine	1947	3,300	154.50	4.68	4.90 [b]	0.15	—		17.10	0.52	12.40	0.37
3	Baton Rouge, Louisiana	1946	34,719	766.53	2.23	57.86	0.16	34.27	0.10	82.20	0.23	75.82	0.22
4	Battle Creek, Michigan	1947	43,453	1,323.00	3.04	223.50	0.51	112.30	0.26	130.70	0.30	154.30	0.36
5	Brookhaven, Mississippi	1950	8,220	404.90	4.93	31.60	0.38	22.60	0.27	26.00	0.32	45.80	0.56
6	Carlsbad, New Mexico	1945	7,116	343.30	4.82	19.10	0.27	9.50	0.13	37.00	0.52	35.60	0.50
7	Centralia, Illinois	1940	17,000	558.60	3.28	6.50	0.04	6.40	0.04	39.90	0.23	4.50	0.03
8	Frankfort, Kentucky	1951	11,916	237.50	1.99	70.30	0.59	39.30	0.33	30.70	0.26	23.40	0.20
9	Freeport, Illinois	1952	22,467	782.90	3.49	101.90	0.45	31.60	0.14	46.90	0.21	53.40	0.24
10	Glasgow, Kentucky	1949	7,040	423.70	6.02	53.00	0.75	20.80	0.30	30.30	0.43	40.50	0.58
11	Jacksonville, Illinois	1950	20,600	930.30	4.52	90.90	0.44	66.30	0.32	49.50	0.24	36.10	0.18
12	Jefferson City, Missouri	1952	23,200	779.90	3.36	103.40	0.45	47.50	0.20	92.50	0.40	51.40	0.22
13	Kankakee, Illinois	1945	22,241	678.40	3.05	133.10	0.60	15.40	0.07	58.90	0.26	33.30	0.15
14	Marshall, Michigan	1950	5,740	399.20	6.95	39.06	0.68	9.71	0.17	28.97	0.50	32.63	0.57
15	Mason City, Iowa	1940	25,500	866.30	3.40	50.70	0.20	23.60	0.09	56.90	0.22	85.40	0.34
16	Mexico, Missouri	1952	12,500	480.40	3.85	51.70	0.42	17.80	0.14	41.30	0.33	31.60	0.25
17	Muskogee, Oklahoma	1945	37,500	1,424.49	3.80	72.94	0.19	25.19	0.07	107.92	0.29	48.24	0.13
18	Naples, Florida	1952	1,740	216.20	12.43	12.70	0.73	14.10	0.81	52.00	2.99	6.30	0.36
19	Petersburg, Virginia	1943	30,631	669.31	2.19	155.92	0.51	35.08	0.12	49.29	0.14	183.98	0.60
20	Quincy, Illinois	1945	42,750	1,275.00	2.98	245.70	0.57	76.80	0.18	87.20	0.20	127.10	0.30
21	Rock Island, Illinois	1940	42,000	1,186.50	2.83	160.90	0.38	45.10	0.11	91.90	0.22	115.90	0.28
22	Roswell, New Mexico	1946	20,400	847.07	4.15	27.14	0.13	17.05	0.08	69.37	0.34	74.16	0.36
23	Santa Fe, New Mexico	1946	24,320	776.72	3.19	19.61	0.08	19.23	0.08	56.98	0.23	53.24	0.22
24	Streator, Illinois	1950	17,268	830.20	4.81	38.20	0.22	10.40	0.06	45.90	0.27	32.10	0.18
25	Tuscola, Illinois	1952	2,967	204.50	6.89	11.50	0.39	2.78	0.09	21.50	0.73	14.22 [d]	0.48
26	West Palm Beach, Florida	1952	44,000	1,165.00	2.65	254.50	0.58	194.90	0.44	266.00	0.60	87.50	0.20

City and Population Group	Area in Acres	Acres Per 100 Persons	Area in Acres	Acres Per 100 Persons	Area in Acres	Acres Per 100 Persons	Area in Acres	Acres Per 100 Persons	Area in Acres	Acres Per 100 Persons	Area in Acres	Acres Per 100 Persons	Area in Acres	
50,000 or Less														
Atchinson, Kansas	13.95	0.11	61.42	0.49	134.19	1.06	69.47	0.55	509.12	4.03	1,430.06	11.31	1,828.48	1
Bar Harbor, Maine	0.00	0.00	0.00	0.00	—	—	44.00 c	1.33	43.80	1.33	276.70	8.38	330.40	2
Baton Rouge, Louisiana	5.84	0.01	235.40	0.68	114.65	0.33	265.61	0.76	662.49	1.91	2,300.67	6.63	3,392.26	3
Battle Creek, Michigan	151.00	0.35	159.60	0.37	288.90	0.66	339.40	0.78	1,040.00	2.39	3,922.70	9.02	6,856.00	4
Brookhaven, Mississippi	33.80	0.41	51.70	0.63	12.50	0.15	67.10	0.82	222.80	2.71	918.80	11.18	1,383.30	5
Carlsbad, New Mexico	7.60	0.11	78.10	1.10	47.10	0.66	56.00	0.79	377.30	5.30	1,010.60	14.20	1,543.10	6
Centralia, Illinois	43.10	0.25	99.80	0.59	3.20	0.02	26.00	0.15	502.60	2.96	1,290.60	7.59	1,775.00	7
Frankfort, Kentucky	14.40	0.12	31.00	0.26	3.70	0.03	215.80	1.81	212.50	1.78	878.60	7.37	1,276.20	8
Freeport, Illinois	45.80	0.20	132.90	0.59	40.80	0.18	146.70	0.65	513.90	2.29	1,896.80	8.44	2,670.30	9
Glasgow, Kentucky	9.40	0.13	7.70	0.11	1.40	0.02	94.70	1.34	147.00	2.09	828.50	11.77	1,432.00	10
Jacksonville, Illinois	32.20	0.16	78.40	0.38	10.70	0.05	387.00	1.88	470.50	2.28	2,151.90	10.45	3,120.50	11
Jefferson City, Missouri	26.50	0.11	98.00	0.42	253.40	1.09	462.90	2.00	663.40	2.86	2,578.90	11.11	6,089.00	12
Kankakee, Illinois	58.90	0.26	115.20	0.52	89.60	0.40	81.90	0.37	770.60	3.46	2,035.30	9.14	2,560.00	13
Marshall, Michigan	58.25	1.01	29.45	0.51	8.01	0.14	245.61	4.28	268.38	4.68	1,119.27	19.49	2,323.80	14
Mason City, Iowa	382.20	1.50	358.10	1.40	41.40	0.16	267.10	1.05	880.10	3.45	3,011.80	11.81	7,995.40	15
Mexico, Missouri	159.00	1.27	91.60	0.73	101.00	0.81	490.20	3.92	422.70	3.38	1,887.30	15.10	4,286.90	16
Muskogee, Oklahoma	13.66	0.04	213.61	0.57	192.98	0.51	549.32	1.46	1,361.01	3.63	4,009.36	10.69	5,795.25	17
Naples, Florida	8.10	0.47	57.60	3.31	10.70	0.61	165.00	9.48	282.90	16.26	825.60	47.45	6,540.00	18
Petersburg, Virginia	37.59	0.13	73.86	0.24	528.75	1.73	273.36	0.89	526.78	1.72	2,533.92	8.27	3,607.67	19
Quincy, Illinois	87.30	0.20	62.30	0.15	182.50	0.43	167.30	0.39	986.60	2.31	3,297.80	7.71	3,795.00	20
Rock Island, Illinois	105.30	0.25	143.40	0.34	120.80	0.29	283.40	0.67	879.30	2.09	3,132.50	7.46	5,297.80	21
Roswell, New Mexico	111.48	0.55	39.14	0.19	53.90	0.26	960.09	4.72	836.36	4.10	3,035.76	14.88	4,291.89	22
Santa Fe, New Mexico	0.00	0.00	22.63	0.09	64.46	0.27	604.80	2.49	552.19	2.27	2,169.86	8.92	16,551.30	23
Streator, Illinois	109.70	0.60	143.90	0.83	25.30	0.15	46.50	0.27	535.80	3.10	1,812.00	10.49	2,192.00	24
Tuscola, Illinois	—	—	18.50	0.62	25.00	0.84	52.00	1.75	166.00	5.60	516.00	17.39	621.00	25
West Palm Beach, Florida	51.10	0.12	250.20	0.57	410.30	0.93	274.00	0.62	1,143.20	2.60	4,096.70	9.31	9,018.50	26
Williamsburg, Virginia	8.20	0.23	20.60	0.59	2.90	0.08	607.40	17.35	193.00	5.51	1,130.10	32.28	1,830.50	27
Woodward, Oklahoma	6.03	0.10	67.60	1.08	21.32	0.34	36.48	0.58	394.65	6.29	836.82	13.34	1,095.44	28

a Estimated, or interpolated from U.S. Census. b Includes multifamily dwelling areas. c Includes parks and playgrounds. d Includes heavy industry. e Includes railroad property.

TABLE 2 (continued). LAND USE IN 53 CENTRAL CITIES. Acres per 100 persons occupied by major urban uses.

City and Population Group	Year of Survey	Population At Date of Survey [a]	Single-Family Dwellings		Two-Family Dwellings		Multi-Family Dwellings		Commercial Use		Light Industry	
			Area in Acres	Acres Per 100 Persons	Area in Acres	Acres Per 100 Persons	Area in Acres	Acres Per 100 Persons	Area in Acres	Acres Per 100 Persons	Area in Acres	Acres Per 100 Persons
50,000 - 100,000												
29 Binghampton, New York	1948	85,397	1,129.00	1.32	552.90	0.65	171.70	0.20	162.30	0.19	227.60	0.27
30 Davenport, Iowa	1945	75,000	2,491.00	3.32	132.00	0.18	85.00	0.11	116.00	0.16	104.00	0.14
31 Decatur, Illinois	1938	57,500	1,909.50	3.32	64.60	0.11	30.60	0.05	124.30	0.22	57.50	0.10
32 Greenville, South Carolina	1950	57,932	2,262.20	3.90	252.00	0.44	276.60	0.48	205.00	0.35	127.60	0.22
33 Hamilton, Ohio	1947	54,500	1,382.00	2.54	146.30	0.27	52.80	0.10	95.10	0.17	110.80	0.20
34 Lansing, Michigan	1937	83,500	1,962.40	2.35	116.10	0.14	36.10	0.04	131.20	0.16	198.10	0.24
35 Lincoln, Nebraska	1951	97,423	3,084.00	3.17	123.00	0.13	142.00	0.15	182.00	0.19	156.00	0.16
36 Portsmouth, Virginia	1946	81,957	653.00	0.80	319.20	0.39	118.80	0.14	81.00	0.10	79.60	0.10
37 Racine, Wisconsin	1938	72,000	1,114.00	1.55	311.70	0.43	40.30	0.05	163.40	0.23	69.50	0.09
38 St. Petersburg, Florida	1941	60,812	2,368.80	3.89	155.40	0.26	272.90	0.45	185.70	0.31	65.30	0.11
39 Sioux Falls, South Dakota	1949	51,000	1,357.10	2.66	105.80	0.21	116.50	0.23	148.80	0.29	127.30	0.25
40 Schenectady, New York	1945	87,549	1,055.30	1.21	650.30	0.74	164.30	0.19	205.60	0.24	130.60	0.15
41 Topeka, Kansas	1942	67,802	2,334.50	3.44	144.80	0.22	87.70	0.13	127.50	0.19	110.00	0.16
100,000 - 250,000												
42 Corpus Christi, Texas	1951	110,900	3,603.20	3.25	182.60	0.16	249.20	0.22	458.90	0.41	282.60	0.25
43 Des Moines, Iowa	1939	153,000	7,035.10	4.60	111.60	0.07	377.10	0.25	415.90	0.27	228.90	0.15
44 Kansas City, Kansas	1938	125,000	3,257.50	2.61	157.40	0.13	66.60	0.05	216.70	0.17	132.90	0.11
45 Oklahoma City, Oklahoma	1945	226,000	5,484.84	2.43	640.71	0.28	267.01	0.12	350.24	0.15	285.36	0.13
46 Richmond, Virginia	1942	193,042	4,487.80	2.33	604.00	0.31	337.60	0.17	412.40	0.21	648.50	0.34
47 Utica, New York	1948	106,750	1,072.60	1.01	667.00	0.62	279.00	0.26	278.00	0.26	171.00	0.16
48 Wichita, Kansas	1944	114,966	4,483.40	3.90	591.50	0.51	249.80	0.22	261.70	0.23	203.90	0.18
250,000 And Over												
49 Dallas, Texas	1944	338,000	9,305.00	2.75	2,143.75	0.64	813.40	0.24	608.33	0.18	382.61	0.11
50 Dayton, Ohio	1952	255,474	5,446.00	2.13	768.00	0.30	443.00	0.17	811.00	0.32	948.00	0.37
51 Memphis, Tennessee	1939	260,000	7,432.20	2.86	865.10	0.33	498.30	0.19	582.40	0.22	922.90	0.36
52 ... New Jersey	1945	(39,760)	1,044.50	0.24	825.00	0.19	1,033.00	0.24	791.00	0.18	356.00	0.08

	City and Population Group	Industry Area in Acres	Acres Per 100 Persons	Area in Acres	Acres Per 100 Persons	Area in Acres	Acres Per 100 Persons	Area in Acres	Acres Per 100 Persons	Area in Acres	Acres Per 100 Persons	Area in Acres	Acres Per 100 Persons	Area in Acres	
	50,000 – 100,000														
29	Binghamton, New York	61.10	0.07	234.10	0.27	469.80	0.55	593.00	0.69	851.70	1.00	4,453.20	5.21	6,919.00	29
30	Davenport, Iowa	114.00	0.15	254.00	0.34	794.00	1.06	722.00	0.96	1,690.00	2.25	6,502.00	8.67	12,911.00	30
31	Decatur, Illinois	208.40	0.35	240.30	0.42	285.20	0.50	195.00	0.34	1,122.50	1.95	4,231.90	7.36	5,192.80	31
32	Greenville, South Carolina	60.60	0.10	160.10	0.28	150.50	0.26	746.30	1.29	1,295.10	2.24	5,536.00	9.56	9,994.00	32
33	Hamilton, Ohio	203.00	0.37	150.00	0.28	315.00	0.58	308.20	0.57	978.40	1.79	3,741.60	6.87	4,499.10	33
34	Lansing, Michigan	344.80	0.41	192.90	0.23	535.20	0.64	465.30	0.56	1,582.90	1.89	5,565.00	6.66	7,659.50	34
35	Lincoln, Nebraska	52.00	0.05	716.00	0.73	385.00	0.39	1,064.00	1.09	4,301.00	4.41	10,205.00	10.47	14,535.00	35
36	Portsmouth, Virginia	71.90	0.09	479.30	0.58	17.50	0.02	324.20	0.40	820.70	1.00	2,965.20	3.62	4,168.30	36
37	Racine, Wisconsin	228.80 [e]	0.32	—	—	444.50	0.62	293.10	0.41	1,250.60	1.74	3,915.90	5.44	5,697.50	37
38	St. Petersburg, Florida	43.40	0.07	251.00	0.41	372.20	0.61	950.50	1.56	6,267.50	10.31	10,932.70	17.98	33,522.20	38
39	Sioux Falls, South Dakota	142.40	0.28	336.00	0.66	499.80	0.98	1,371.50	2.69	1,588.10	3.11	5,793.30	11.36	7,931.00	39
40	Schenectady, New York	423.50	0.48	217.90	0.25	427.20	0.49	739.00	0.84	1,070.90	1.22	5,084.60	5.81	6,643.30	40
41	Topeka, Kansas	68.00	0.10	394.50	0.58	181.40	0.27	313.60	0.46	2,041.00	3.01	5,803.00	8.56	7,468.00	41
	100,000 – 250,000														
42	Corpus Christi, Texas	410.30	0.37	149.60	0.14	197.70	0.18	1,050.10	0.95	2,634.20	2.38	9,218.40	8.31	81,191.00	42
43	Des Moines, Iowa	418.20	0.27	948.80	0.62	1,003.70	0.66	2,807.30	1.83	4,450.10	2.91	17,796.70	11.63	35,530.50	43
44	Kansas City, Kansas	632.90	0.51	1,128.30	0.90	309.50	0.25	430.20	0.34	2,512.70	2.01	8,844.70	7.08	13,007.70	44
45	Oklahoma City, Oklahoma	354.23	0.16	516.84	0.23	878.13	0.39	780.01	0.34	4,281.61	1.89	13,838.98	6.12	16,852.18	45
46	Richmond, Virginia	501.20	0.26	738.70	0.38	1,029.20	0.53	2,064.70	1.07	4,165.00	2.16	14,989.10	7.76	25,430.70	46
47	Utica, New York	374.00	0.35	622.50	0.58	665.70	0.62	1,171.20	1.10	1,298.30	1.22	6,599.30	6.18	10,387.00	47
48	Wichita, Kansas	182.10	0.16	353.10	0.31	608.40	0.53	971.90	0.84	3,437.50	2.99	11,343.30	9.87	14,326.00	48
	250,000 And Over														
49	Dallas, Texas	413.66	0.12	722.06	0.21	4,020.37	1.19	1,424.70	0.42	6,276.96	1.86	26,110.84	7.72	32,162.61	49
50	Dayton, Ohio	133.00	0.05	334.00	0.13	478.00	0.19	1,403.00	0.55	3,651.00	1.43	14,415.00	5.64	17,337.00	50
51	Memphis, Tennessee	987.00	0.38	1,098.50	0.42	1,128.80	0.43	1,656.10	0.64	4,652.90	1.79	19,824.20	7.62	31,133.40	51
52	Newark, New Jersey	1,702.50	0.40	771.00	0.18	790.00	0.18	2,209.00	0.52	2,858.80	0.67	12,380.80	2.88	16,435.20	52
53	St. Louis, Missouri	1,752.00	0.21	1,723.90	0.21	2,698.80	0.33	3,485.50	0.42	8,836.00	1.08	33,440.90	4.07	39,836.00	53

[a] Estimated, or interpolated from U.S. Census. [b] Includes multifamily dwelling areas. [c] Includes parks and playgrounds. [d] Includes heavy industry. [e] Includes railroad property.

TABLE 3. SUMMARY OF LAND USE IN 53 CENTRAL CITIES.

Percentage of total developed area and total city area occupied by major urban uses, by city size classes.

| Use | Population Group | | | | | | | | | | | | | | |
| | Less than 50,000 28 Cities | | | 50,000 - 100,000 13 Cities | | | 100,000 - 250,000 7 Cities | | | 250,000 & Over 5 Cities | | | Total All 53 Cities | | |
	Area in Acres	% of Developed Area	% of City Area	Area in Acres	% of Developed Area	% of City Area	Area in Acres	% of Developed Area	% of City Area	Area in Acres	% of Developed Area	% of City Area	Area in Acres	% of Developed Area	% of City Area
Single-Family Dwellings	18,719.87	34.08	17.10	23,102.80	30.92	18.17	29,424.44	35.61	14.96	30,044.70	28.30	21.94	101,291.81	31.81	17.76
Two-Family Dwellings	2,058.99	3.75	1.88	3,074.10	4.11	2.42	2,954.81	3.58	1.50	7,183.75	6.77	5.25	15,271.65	4.79	2.68
Multifamily Dwellings	953.60	1.73	0.87	1,595.30	2.13	1.25	1,826.31	2.21	0.93	5,212.20	4.90	3.81	9,587.41	3.01	1.68
Commercial Areas	1,726.44	3.14	1.58	1,927.90	2.58	1.52	2,393.84	2.90	1.22	4,528.03	4.26	3.31	10,576.21	3.32	1.85
Light Industry	1,526.33	2.78	1.39	1,563.90	2.09	1.23	1,953.16	2.36	0.99	3,995.51	3.76	2.92	9,038.90	2.84	1.59
Heavy Industry	1,574.40	2.87	1.44	2,015.90	2.70	1.59	2,872.93	3.48	1.46	4,988.16	4.70	3.64	11,451.39	3.60	2.01
Railroad Property	2,741.71	4.99	2.50	3,626.10	4.85	2.85	4,457.84	5.39	2.27	4,649.46	4.38	3.40	15,475.11	4.86	2.71
Parks and Playgrounds	2,789.46	5.08	2.55	4,877.30	6.53	3.84	4,692.33	5.68	2.38	9,115.97	8.59	6.66	21,475.06	6.74	3.77
Public and Semipublic Property	7,279.14	13.25	6.65	8,085.70	10.82	6.36	9,275.41	11.22	4.71	10,178.30	9.59	7.43	34,818.55	10.93	6.11
Streets	15,564.98	28.33	14.21	24,860.40	33.27	19.55	22,779.41	27.57	11.58	26,275.66	24.75	19.19	89,480.45	28.10	15.69
Total Developed Area	54,934.92	100.00	50.17	74,729.40	100.00	58.78	82,630.48	100.00	42.00	106,171.74	100.00	77.55	318,466.54	100.00	55.85
Vacant Areas	51,474.19	-	47.01	49,335.80	-	38.80	42,979.90	-	21.85	27,884.94	-	20.37	171,674.83	-	30.10
Water Areas	3,089.88	-	2.82	3,075.50	-	2.42	71,114.70	-	36.15	2,847.53	-	2.08	80,127.61	-	14.05
Total Surveyed Area	109,498.99	-	100.00	127,140.70	-	100.00	196,725.08	-	100.00	136,904.21	-	100.00	570,268.98	-	100.00

Population Group

Use	Less than 50,000 28 Cities		50,000 - 100,000 13 Cities		100,000 - 250,000 7 Cities		250,000 & Over 5 Cities		Total All 53 Cities	
	Area in Acres	Acres Per 100 Persons	Area in Acres	Acres Per 100 Persons	Area in Acres	Acres Per 100 Persons	Area in Acres	Acres Per 100 Persons	Area in Acres	Acres Per 100 Persons
Single-Family Dwellings	18,719.87	3.40	23,102.80	2.48	29,424.44	2.86	30,044.70	1.43	101,291.81	2.19
Two-Family Dwellings	2,058.99	0.37	3,074.10	0.33	2,954.81	0.29	7,183.75	0.34	15,271.65	0.33
Multifamily Dwellings	953.60	0.17	1,595.30	0.17	1,826.31	0.18	5,212.20	0.25	9,587.41	0.21
Commercial Areas	1,726.44	0.31	1,927.90	0.21	2,393.84	0.23	4,528.03	0.21	10,576.21	0.23
Light Industry	1,526.33	0.28	1,563.90	0.17	1,953.16	0.19	3,995.51	0.19	9,038.90	0.20
Heavy Industry	1,574.40	0.29	2,015.90	0.21	2,872.93	0.28	4,988.16	0.24	11,451.39	0.25
Railroad Property	2,741.71	0.50	3,626.10	0.39	4,457.84	0.43	4,649.46	0.22	15,475.11	0.33
Parks and Playgrounds	2,789.46	0.51	4,877.30	0.52	4,692.33	0.46	9,115.97	0.43	21,475.06	0.46
Public and Semipublic Property	7,279.14	1.32	8,085.70	0.87	9,275.41	0.90	10,178.30	0.48	34,818.55	0.75
Streets	15,564.98	2.82	24,860.40	2.66	22,779.41	2.21	26,275.66	1.25	89,480.45	1.94
Total Developed Area	54,934.92	9.97	74,729.40	8.01	82,630.48	8.03	106,171.74	5.04	318,466.54	6.89
Total Surveyed Area	109,498.99	-	127,140.70	-	196,725.08	-	136,904.21	-	570,268.98	-

TABLE 5.   LAND USE IN 33 SATELLITE CITIES

	City And Population Group	Year Of Survey	Population[a] At Date Of Survey	Single Family Dwellings			Two Family Dwellings		% O
				Area In Acres	% Of Total Developed Area	% Of Total City Area	Area In Acres	% Of Total Developed Area	
	5,000 or Less								
1	Berkeley, Missouri	1941	3,100	110.20	26.99	3.79	0.10	0.03	
2	Bettendorf, Iowa	1947	4,022	176.40	28.00	8.83	2.90	0.46	
3	Glendale, Ohio	1942	2,359	406.58	65.52	40.14	17.49	2.82	
4	Lincolnwood, Illinois	1945	2,450	89.47	11.16	5.14	5.57	0.69	
5	Morton Grove, Illinois	1945	3,150	104.08	8.33	3.97	8.89	0.71	
6	Northfield, Illinois	1942	900	157.11	29.63	12.61	3.30	0.62	
7	Olivette, Missouri	1940	1,130	176.20	46.42	14.08	3.80	1.00	
	5,000 - 10,000								
8	Edwardsville, Illinois	1945	8,008	422.00	44.90	29.83	3.20	0.34	
9	Falls Church, Virginia	1950	8,343	631.30	60.67	48.35	15.70	1.51	
10	Ferguson, Missouri	1945	7,299	837.31	64.93	42.91	8.82	0.68	
11	Skokie, Illinois	1945	9,700	261.10	9.43	4.00	26.10	0.94	
12	West Vancouver, British Columbia	1946	8,545	996.00	30.26	18.48	17.70	0.54	
13	Wyoming, Ohio	1946	5,231	441.50	57.48	41.78	35.60	4.64	
	10,000 - 25,000								
14	Brentwood, Missouri	1952	12,500	415.10	45.83	29.54	3.90	0.43	
15	Clayton, Missouri	1941	13,069	547.22	44.22	34.27	27.25	2.20	
16	Highland Park, Illinois	1946	15,300	1,425.75	37.05	18.32	67.63	1.76	
17	Kirkwood, Missouri	1941	11,389	1,056.28	51.06	25.25	9.55	0.46	
18	La Grange, Illinois	1939	10,000	384.40	42.12	31.01	27.00	2.96	
19	Richmond Heights, Missouri	1941	12,754	547.70	60.11	39.66	40.20	4.41	
20	University Park, Texas	1940	16,000	721.70	48.70	32.85	85.40	5.76	
21	Webster Groves, Missouri	1937	16,487	1,497.70	63.17	47.43	16.50	0.70	
22	Wilmette, Illinois	1939	14,900	817.00	38.79	23.98	43.30	2.05	
23	Winnetka, Illinois	1940	13,000	1,159.00	55.75	47.28	0.00	0.00	
	25,000 And Over								
24	Beverley Hills, California	1947	28,669	1,451.59	53.32	45.09	68.30	2.51	
25	Bloomfield, New Jersey	1948	44,165	865.00	31.75	25.03	174.90	6.42	
26	East Chicago, Indiana	1945	54,637	342.40	7.14	5.00	157.50	3.28	
27	East Orange, New Jersey	1945	68,945	747.25	32.99	29.70	262.67	11.60	
28	East St. Louis, Illinois	1936	74,347	1,538.60	30.84	19.85	234.60	4.70	
29	Evanston, Illinois	1939	70,900	1,339.20	33.21	27.50	159.60	3.96	
30	Irvington, New Jersey	1948	60,199	440.70	24.78	22.54	257.40	14.47	
31	Maywood, Illinois	1950	26,648	567.44	36.59	31.94	109.20	7.04	
32	New Westminster, British Columbia	1946	25,000	744.80	30.31	19.66	6.40	0.26	
33	Oak Park, Illinois	1946	70,372	1,326.10	45.71	44.11	180.00	6.20	

[a]Estimated, or interpolated from U. S. Census.

age of total developed area and total city area occupied by major urban uses.

Multiple Dwellings		Commercial Use			Light and Heavy Industry			Railroad Property		
% Of Total Developed Area	% Of Total City Area	Area In Acres	% Of Total Developed Area	% Of Total City Area	Area in Acres	% of Total Developed Area	% of Total City Area	Area in Acres	% of Total Developed Area	% of Total City Area
0.00	0.00	4.70	1.15	0.16	11.80	2.89	0.41	37.00	9.06	1.27
0.30	0.09	10.30	1.63	0.52	185.70	29.47	9.30	48.50	7.70	2.43
0.61	0.37	3.73	0.60	0.37	1.55	0.25	0.15	9.50	1.53	0.94
0.00	0.00	37.14	4.63	2.13	50.93	6.35	2.92	28.17	3.51	1.62
0.09	0.05	66.74	5.34	2.54	20.37	1.63	0.78	19.79	1.58	0.75
0.03	0.01	8.49	1.60	0.68	24.66	4.65	1.98	47.74	9.00	3.83
0.00	0.00	9.10	2.40	0.73	7.90	2.08	0.63	18.60	4.90	1.49
0.38	0.25	27.60	2.94	1.95	51.30	5.46	3.63	45.00	4.79	3.18
4.94	3.94	33.60	3.23	2.57	10.20	0.98	0.78	20.10	1.93	1.54
0.06	0.04	9.84	0.76	0.50	23.17	1.80	1.19	31.45	2.44	1.61
0.71	0.30	45.70	1.65	0.70	137.10	4.95	2.10	163.20	5.90	2.50
0.08	0.05	16.60	0.51	0.31	6.20	0.19	0.11	124.00	3.77	2.30
1.84	1.33	11.40	1.48	1.08	23.30	3.03	2.21	3.10	0.40	0.29
12.06	7.77	30.10	3.32	2.14	116.30	12.84	8.28	7.20	0.80	0.51
5.21	4.04	35.79	2.89	2.24	5.28	0.43	0.33	38.14	3.08	2.39
0.33	0.16	92.84	2.41	1.19	41.43	1.07	0.53	183.07	4.76	2.36
0.42	0.21	39.55	1.91	0.95	13.97	0.68	0.33	100.08	4.84	2.39
1.06	0.78	20.90	2.29	1.69	37.80	4.14	3.06	29.80	3.26	2.40
3.79	2.50	15.90	1.74	1.15	3.10	0.34	0.22	14.80	1.62	1.07
1.40	0.95	15.50	1.05	0.71	0.50	0.03	0.02	2.60	0.18	0.12
0.18	0.14	39.60	1.67	1.25	34.50	1.46	1.09	83.80	3.53	2.65
0.27	0.17	62.10	2.95	1.82	26.90	1.28	0.79	38.30	1.82	1.12
0.38	0.32	22.80	1.10	0.93	6.30	0.30	0.26	45.50	2.19	1.86
4.57	3.87	148.69	5.46	4.62	27.69	1.02	0.86	19.50	0.72	0.61
3.25	2.56	69.10	2.54	2.00	289.90	10.64	8.39	0.00	0.00	0.00
2.14	1.50	61.60	1.28	0.90	2,595.39	54.08	37.90	616.30	12.84	9.00
12.19	10.98	106.11	4.68	4.22	93.31	4.12	3.71	33.22	1.47	1.32
1.21	0.78	186.70	3.74	2.41	412.10	8.26	5.32	695.70	13.94	8.97
3.91	3.23	91.20	2.26	1.87	176.10	4.37	3.61	191.20	4.74	3.93
9.43	8.58	113.60	6.39	5.81	167.40	9.41	8.56	29.60	1.67	1.51
3.56	3.10	37.17	2.40	2.09	115.75	7.46	6.52	49.95	3.22	2.81
0.41	0.26	37.00	1.50	0.98	179.60	7.31	4.74	99.70	4.06	2.63
4.98	4.81	86.68	2.99	2.88	41.88	1.45	1.39	49.81	1.72	1.66

TABLE 5 (continued).   LAND USE IN 33 SATELLITE CITIES.

	City And Population Group	Parks & Playgrounds			Public & Semi-Public Property		
		Area in Acres	% of Total Developed Area	% of Total City Area	Area in Acres	% of Total Developed Area	% of Total City Area
	5,000 or Less						
1	Berkeley, Missouri	2.00	0.49	0.07	47.50	11.63	1.63
2	Bettendorf, Iowa	6.40	1.02	0.32	9.70	1.54	0.49
3	Glendale, Ohio	11.51	1.85	1.14	71.46	11.51	7.05
4	Lincolnwood, Illinois	0.00	0.00	0.00	193.54	24.13	11.11
5	Morton Grove, Illinois	0.63	0.05	0.02	642.55	51.42	24.49
6	Northfield, Illinois	117.88	22.23	9.47	3.74	0.70	0.30
7	Olivette, Missouri	0.00	0.00	0.00	87.90	23.15	7.03
	5,000 - 10,000						
8	Edwardsville, Illinois	54.60	5.81	3.86	47.00	5.00	3.32
9	Falls Church, Virginia	0.00	0.00	0.00	63.70	6.12	4.88
10	Ferguson, Missouri	0.00	0.00	0.00	162.35	12.59	8.32
11	Skokie, Illinois	39.20	1.42	0.60	620.20	22.41	9.50
12	West Vancouver, British Columbia	617.00	18.74	11.45	451.10	13.70	8.37
13	Wyoming, Ohio	1.50	0.20	0.14	120.30	15.66	11.39
	10,000 - 25,000						
14	Brentwood, Missouri	11.80	1.30	0.84	35.90	3.96	2.56
15	Clayton, Missouri	50.65	4.09	3.17	179.02	14.47	11.21
16	Highland Park, Illinois	225.39	5.86	2.90	897.73	23.33	11.54
17	Kirkwood, Missouri	6.43	0.31	0.15	268.59	12.98	6.42
18	La Grange, Illinois	26.70	2.93	2.15	41.60	4.56	3.36
19	Richmond Heights, Missouri	4.40	0.48	0.32	32.50	3.57	2.36
20	University Park, Texas	24.00	1.62	1.09	147.10	9.93	6.70
21	Webster Groves, Missouri	11.40	0.48	0.36	269.50	11.37	8.53
22	Wilmette, Illinois	131.30	6.23	3.85	321.80	15.28	9.44
23	Winnetka, Illinois	341.40	16.42	13.93	90.80	4.37	3.70
	25,000 And Over						
24	Beverley Hills, California	49.65	1.82	1.54	64.66	2.38	2.01
25	Bloomfield, New Jersey	170.40	6.26	4.93	546.10	20.04	15.80
26	East Chicago, Indiana	143.10	2.98	2.09	109.56	2.28	1.60
27	East Orange, New Jersey	42.52	1.88	1.69	161.93	7.15	6.44
28	East St. Louis, Illinois	197.80	3.96	2.55	111.10	2.23	1.43
29	Evanston, Illinois	101.80	2.53	2.09	555.00	13.76	11.40
30	Irvington, New Jersey	79.90	4.49	4.09	84.10	4.73	4.30
31	Maywood, Illinois	26.68	1.72	1.50	71.69	4.62	4.03
32	New Westminster, British Columbia	185.30	7.54	4.89	270.60	11.01	7.15
33	Oak Park, Illinois	62.43	2.15	2.08	91.00	3.14	3.03

Streets			Vacant Areas		Water Areas		Total Developed Area	Total City Area	
Area in Acres	% of Total Developed Area	% of Total City Area	Area in Acres	% of Total City Area	Area in Acres	% of Total City Area	Area in Acres	Area in Acres	
495.00	47.76	6.70	2,501.50	85.97	0.00	0.00	408.30	2,909.80	1
488.30	29.88	9.43	939.60	47.05	427.20	21.39	630.10	1,996.90	2
95.00	15.31	9.38	392.28	38.73	0.00	0.00	620.58	1,012.86	3
397.27	49.53	22.80	939.91	53.96	0.00	0.00	802.09	1,742.00	4
385.49	30.85	14.69	1,374.28	52.37	0.00	0.00	1,249.72	2,624.00	5
167.24	31.54	13.43	715.20	57.42	0.00	0.00	530.31	1,245.51	6
76.10	20.05	6.08	871.40	69.66	0.00	0.00	379.60	1,251.00	7
285.50	30.38	20.18	475.10	33.58	0.00	0.00	939.80	1,414.90	8
214.50	20.62	16.43	265.10	20.31	0.00	0.00	1,040.50	1,305.60	9
215.94	16.74	11.07	661.83	33.91	0.00	0.00	1,289.61	1,951.44	10
455.70	52.59	22.30	3,760.20	57.60	0.00	0.00	2,767.80	6,528.00	11
060.40	32.21	19.67	2,098.30	38.93	0.00	0.00	3,291.70	5,390.00	12
117.30	15.27	11.10	288.60	27.31	0.00	0.00	768.10	1,056.70	13
176.30	19.46	12.55	499.20	35.53	0.00	0.00	905.80	1,405.00	14
289.72	23.41	18.14	359.33	22.50	0.00	0.00	1,237.51	1,596.84	15
901.68	23.43	11.59	3,931.73	50.54	0.00	0.00	3,848.27	7,780.00	16
565.47	27.34	13.52	2,114.62	50.55	0.00	0.00	2,068.58	4,183.20	17
334.70	36.68	27.00	326.90	26.37	0.00	0.00	912.60	1,239.50	18
218.10	23.94	15.79	469.80	34.02	0.00	0.00	911.20	1,381.00	19
464.20	31.33	21.13	714.90	32.54	0.00	0.00	1,481.80	2,196.70	20
413.60	17.44	13.10	787.20	24.93	0.00	0.00	2,370.90	3,158.10	21
659.90	31.33	19.37	1,301.30	38.19	0.00	0.00	2,106.40	3,407.70	22
405.30	19.49	16.53	372.50	15.19	0.00	0.00	2,079.00	2,451.50	23
767.81	28.20	23.85	496.82	15.43	0.00	0.00	2,722.27	3,219.09	24
520.50	19.10	15.06	731.60	21.17	0.00	0.00	2,724.40	3,456.00	25
671.00	13.98	9.80	1,829.12	26.71	219.13	3.20	4,799.65	6,847.90	26
542.17	23.93	21.55	250.40	9.95	0.00	0.00	2,265.26	2,515.66	27
552.50	31.12	20.03	2,761.60	35.63	0.00	0.00	4,989.40	7,751.00	28
260.50	31.26	25.89	837.40	17.20	0.00	0.00	4,032.10	4,869.50	29
437.90	24.63	22.39	177.10	9.06	0.00	0.00	1,778.30	1,955.40	30
517.96	33.39	29.15	209.06	11.77	16.70	0.94	1,551.01	1,776.77	31
924.20	37.60	24.40	1,330.10	35.12	0.00	0.00	2,457.60	3,787.70	32
918.46	31.66	30.55	105.35	3.50	0.00	0.00	2,900.82	3,006.17	33

TABLE 6. LAND USE IN 33 SATELLITE CITIES.

	City and Population Group	Year of Survey	Population[a] At Date of Survey	Single Family Dwellings		Two Family Dwellings		Mult Dwel
				Area in Acres	Acres Per 100 Persons	Area in Acres	Acres Per 100 Persons	Area in Acres
	5,000 or Less							
1	Berkeley, Missouri	1941	3,100	110.20	3.56	0.10	0.00	0.00
2	Bettendorf, Iowa	1947	4,022	176.40	4.39	2.90	0.07	1.90
3	Glendale, Ohio	1942	2,359	406.58	17.23	17.49	0.74	3.76
4	Lincolnwood, Illinois	1945	2,450	89.47	3.65	5.57	0.23	0.00
5	Morton Grove, Illinois	1945	3,150	104.08	3.30	8.89	0.28	1.18
6	Northfield, Illinois	1942	900	157.11	17.46	3.30	0.37	0.15
7	Olivette, Missouri	1940	1,130	176.20	15.59	3.80	0.34	0.00
	5,000 - 10,000							
8	Edwardsville, Illinois	1945	8,008	422.00	5.27	3.20	0.04	3.60
9	Falls Church, Virginia	1950	8,343	631.30	7.57	15.70	0.19	51.40
10	Ferguson, Missouri	1945	7,299	837.31	11.47	8.82	0.12	0.73
11	Skokie, Illinois	1945	9,700	261.10	2.69	26.10	0.27	19.50
12	West Vancouver, British Columbia	1946	8,545	996.00	11.66	17.70	0.21	2.70
13	Wyoming, Ohio	1946	5,231	441.50	8.44	35.60	0.68	14.10
	10,000 - 25,000							
14	Brentwood, Missouri	1952	12,500	415.10	3.32	3.90	0.03	109.20
15	Clayton, Missouri	1941	13,069	547.22	4.19	27.25	0.21	64.44
16	Highland Park, Illinois	1946	15,300	1,425.75	9.32	67.63	0.44	12.75
17	Kirkwood, Missouri	1941	11,389	1,056.28	9.27	9.55	0.08	8.66
18	La Grange, Illinois	1939	10,000	384.40	3.84	27.00	0.27	9.70
19	Richmond Heights, Missouri	1941	12,754	547.70	4.29	40.20	0.31	34.50
20	University Park, Texas	1940	16,000	721.70	4.51	85.40	0.53	20.80
21	Webster Groves, Missouri	1937	16,487	1,497.70	9.08	16.50	0.10	4.30
22	Wilmette, Illinois	1939	14,900	817.00	5.48	43.30	0.29	5.80
23	Winnetka, Illinois	1940	13,000	1,159.00	8.92	0.00	0.00	7.90
	25,000 and Over							
24	Beverly Hills, California	1947	28,669	1,451.59	5.06	68.30	0.24	124.38
25	Bloomfield, New Jersey	1948	44,165	865.00	1.96	174.90	0.40	88.50
26	East Chicago, Indiana	1945	54,637	342.40	0.62	157.50	0.29	102.80
27	East Orange, New Jersey	1945	68,945	747.25	1.08	262.67	0.38	276.08
28	East St. Louis, Illinois	1936	74,347	1,538.60	2.07	234.60	0.32	60.30
29	Evanston, Illinois	1939	70,900	1,339.20	1.89	159.60	0.23	157.50
30	Irvington, New Jersey	1948	60,199	440.70	0.73	257.40	0.43	167.70
31	Maywood, Illinois	1950	26,648	567.44	2.13	109.20	0.41	55.17
32	New Westminster, British Columbia	1946	25,000	744.80	2.98	6.40	0.02	10.00
33	Oak Park, Illinois	1946	70,372	1,326.10	1.88	180.00	0.26	144.46

[a]Estimated, or interpolated from U. S. Census.

Acres per 100 persons occupied by major urban uses.

Commercial Use		Light and Heavy Industry		Railroad Property		Parks and Playgrounds		Public and Semi-Public Property	
Area in Acres	Acres Per 100 Persons	Area in Acres	Acres Per 100 Persons	Area in Acres	Acres Per 100 Persons	Area in Acres	Acres Per 100 Persons	Area in Acres	Acres Per 100 Persons
4.70	0.15	11.80	0.39	37.00	1.19	2.00	0.06	47.50	1.53
10.30	0.26	185.70	4.62	48.50	1.20	6.40	0.16	9.70	0.24
3.73	0.16	1.55	0.07	9.50	0.40	11.51	0.49	71.46	3.03
37.14	1.52	50.93	2.08	28.17	1.15	0.00	0.00	193.54	7.90
66.74	2.12	20.37	0.65	19.79	0.63	0.63	0.02	642.55	20.40
8.49	0.94	24.66	2.74	47.74	5.30	117.88	13.10	3.74	0.41
9.10	0.80	7.90	0.70	18.60	1.65	0.00	0.00	87.90	7.78
27.60	0.34	51.30	0.64	45.00	0.56	54.60	0.68	47.00	0.59
33.60	0.40	10.20	0.12	20.10	0.24	0.00	0.00	63.70	0.76
9.84	0.14	23.17	0.32	31.45	0.43	0.00	0.00	162.35	2.22
45.70	0.47	137.10	1.41	163.20	1.68	39.20	0.41	620.20	6.39
16.60	0.19	6.20	0.07	124.00	1.45	617.00	7.22	451.10	5.28
11.40	0.22	23.30	0.44	3.10	0.06	1.50	0.03	120.30	2.30
30.10	0.24	116.30	0.93	7.20	0.06	11.80	0.09	35.90	0.29
35.79	0.27	5.28	0.04	38.14	0.29	50.65	0.39	179.02	1.37
92.84	0.61	41.43	0.27	183.07	1.20	225.39	1.47	897.73	5.87
39.55	0.35	13.97	0.12	100.08	0.88	6.43	0.06	268.59	2.36
20.90	0.21	37.80	0.37	29.80	0.30	26.70	0.27	41.60	0.42
15.90	0.12	3.10	0.04	14.80	0.12	4.40	0.03	32.50	0.25
15.50	0.10	0.50	0.00	2.60	0.02	24.00	0.15	147.10	0.92
39.60	0.24	34.50	0.21	83.80	0.51	11.40	0.07	269.50	1.63
62.10	0.42	26.90	0.18	38.30	0.26	131.30	0.88	321.80	2.16
22.80	0.17	6.30	0.05	45.50	0.35	341.40	2.62	90.80	0.70
148.69	0.52	27.69	0.09	19.50	0.07	49.65	0.17	64.66	0.23
69.10	0.16	289.90	0.65	0.00	0.00	170.40	0.38	546.10	1.24
61.60	0.11	2,595.39	4.75	616.30	1.13	143.10	0.26	109.56	0.20
106.11	0.15	93.31	0.13	33.22	0.05	42.52	0.06	161.93	0.24
186.70	0.25	412.10	0.55	695.70	0.93	197.80	0.27	111.10	0.15
91.20	0.13	176.10	0.25	191.20	0.27	101.80	0.14	555.00	0.78
113.60	0.19	167.40	0.27	29.60	0.05	79.90	0.13	84.10	0.14
37.17	0.14	115.75	0.43	49.95	0.19	26.68	0.10	71.69	0.27
37.00	0.15	179.60	0.72	39.70	0.40	185.30	0.74	270.60	1.08
86.68	0.12	41.88	0.06	49.81	0.07	62.43	0.09	91.00	0.13

TABLE 6 (continued).   LAND USE IN 33 SATELLITE CITIES.

Acres per 100 persons occupied by major urban uses.

	City and Population Group	Streets		Total Developed Area		Total City Area	
		Area in Acres	Acres Per 100 Persons	Area in Acres	Acres Per 100 Persons	Area in Acres	
	5,000 or Less						
1	Berkeley, Missouri	195.00	6.29	408.30	13.17	2,909.80	1
2	Bettendorf, Iowa	188.30	4.68	630.10	15.67	1,996.90	2
3	Glendale, Ohio	95.00	4.03	620.58	26.31	1,012.86	3
4	Lincolnwood, Illinois	397.27	16.21	802.09	32.74	1,742.00	4
5	Morton Grove, Illinois	385.49	12.24	1,249.72	39.67	2,624.00	5
6	Northfield, Illinois	167.24	18.58	530.31	58.92	1,245.51	6
7	Olivette, Missouri	76.10	6.73	379.60	33.59	1,251.00	7
	5,000 - 10,000						
8	Edwardsville, Illinois	285.50	3.57	939.80	11.73	1,414.90	8
9	Falls Church, Virginia	214.50	2.57	1,040.50	12.47	1,305.60	9
10	Ferguson, Missouri	215.94	2.96	1,289.61	17.67	1,951.44	10
11	Skokie, Illinois	1,455.70	15.01	2,767.80	28.53	6,528.00	11
12	West Vancouver, British Columbia	1,060.40	12.41	3,291.70	38.52	5,390.00	12
13	Wyoming, Ohio	117.30	2.24	768.10	14.68	1,056.70	13
	10,000 - 25,000						
14	Brentwood, Missouri	176.30	1.41	905.80	7.24	1,405.00	14
15	Clayton, Missouri	289.72	2.22	1,237.51	9.47	1,596.84	15
16	Highland Park, Illinois	901.68	5.89	3,848.27	25.15	7,780.00	16
17	Kirkwood, Missouri	565.47	4.96	2,068.58	18.16	4,183.20	17
18	La Grange, Illinois	334.70	3.35	912.60	9.13	1,239.50	18
19	Richmond Heights, Missouri	218.10	1.71	911.20	7.14	1,381.00	19
20	University Park, Texas	464.20	2.90	1,481.80	9.26	2,196.70	20
21	Webster Groves, Missouri	413.60	2.51	2,370.90	14.38	3,158.10	21
22	Wilmette, Illinois	659.90	4.43	2,106.40	14.14	3,407.70	22
23	Winnetka, Illinois	405.30	3.12	2,079.00	15.99	2,451.50	23
	25,000 and Over						
24	Beverly Hills, California	767.81	2.68	2,722.27	9.50	3,219.09	24
25	Bloomfield, New Jersey	520.50	1.18	2,724.40	6.17	3,456.00	25
26	East Chicago, Indiana	671.00	1.23	4,799.65	8.78	6,847.90	26
27	East Orange, New Jersey	542.17	0.79	2,265.26	3.28	2,515.66	27
28	East St. Louis, Illinois	1,552.50	2.09	4,989.40	6.71	7,751.00	28
29	Evanston, Illinois	1,260.50	1.78	4,032.10	5.69	4,869.50	29
30	Irvington, New Jersey	437.90	0.73	1,778.30	2.95	1,955.40	30
31	Maywood, Illinois	517.96	1.94	1,551.01	5.82	1,776.77	31
32	New Westminster, British Columbia	924.20	3.70	2,457.60	9.83	3,787.70	32
33	Oak Park, Illinois	918.46	1.30	2,900.82	4.12	3,006.17	33

TABLE 7. SUMMARY OF LAND USE IN 33 SATELLITE CITIES.

Percentage of total developed area and total city area occupied by major urban uses, by city size classes.

| | Population Group | | | | | | | | | | | | | | | Total All 33 Cities | | |
| | Less than 5,000 7 Cities | | | 5,000 - 10,000 6 Cities | | | 10,000 - 25,000 10 Cities | | | 25,000 and Over 10 Cities | | | | | |
Use	Area in Acres	% of Developed Area	% of City Area	Area in Acres	% of Developed Area	% of City Area	Area in Acres	% of Developed Area	% of City Area	Area in Acres	% of Developed Area	% of City Area	Area in Acres	% of Developed Area	% of City Area
Single-Family Dwellings	1,220.04	26.41	9.55	3,589.21	35.55	20.34	8,571.85	47.83	29.76	9,363.08	30.98	23.89	22,744.18	36.18	23.11
Two-Family Dwellings	42.05	0.91	0.33	107.12	1.06	0.61	320.73	1.79	1.11	1,610.57	5.33	4.11	2,080.47	3.31	2.11
Multifamily Dwellings	6.99	0.15	0.05	92.03	0.91	0.52	278.05	1.55	0.97	1,186.89	3.93	3.03	1,563.96	2.49	1.59
Commercial Areas	140.20	3.03	1.10	144.74	1.43	0.82	375.08	2.09	1.30	937.85	3.10	2.39	1,597.87	2.54	1.62
Light and Heavy Industry	302.91	6.55	2.37	251.27	2.49	1.42	286.08	1.60	0.99	4,099.12	13.57	10.46	4,939.38	7.86	5.02
Railroad Property	209.30	4.53	1.64	386.85	3.83	2.19	543.29	3.03	1.89	1,784.98	5.91	4.56	2,924.42	4.65	2.97
Parks and Playgrounds	138.42	3.00	1.08	712.30	7.05	4.04	833.47	4.65	2.90	1,059.58	3.51	2.71	2,743.77	4.37	2.79
Public and Semipublic Property	1,056.39	22.86	8.26	1,464.65	14.51	8.30	2,284.54	12.75	7.93	2,065.74	6.83	5.27	6,871.32	10.93	6.99
Streets	1,504.40	32.56	11.77	3,349.34	33.17	18.98	4,428.97	24.71	15.38	8,113.00	26.84	20.70	17,395.71	27.67	17.68
Total Developed Area	4,620.70	100.00	36.15	10,097.51	100.00	57.22	17,922.06	100.00	62.23	30,220.81	100.00	77.12	62,861.08	100.00	63.88
Vacant Areas	7,734.17	-	60.51	7,549.13	-	42.78	10,877.48	-	37.77	8,728.55	-	22.28	34,889.33	-	35.45
Water Areas	427.20	-	3.34	0.00	-	0.00	0.00	-	0.00	235.83	-	0.60	663.03	-	0.67
Total Surveyed Area	12,782.07	-	100.00	17,646.64	-	100.00	28,799.54	-	100.00	39,185.19	-	100.00	98,413.44	-	100.00

TABLE 8. SUMMARY OF LAND USE IN 33 SATELLITE CITIES. Acres per 100 persons occupied by major urban uses, by city size classes.

Population Group

Use	Less than 5,000 7 Cities		5,000 - 10,000 6 Cities		10,000 - 25,000 10 Cities		25,000 and Over 10 Cities		Total All 33 Cities	
	Area in Acres	Acres Per 100 Persons	Area in Acres	Acres Per 100 Persons	Area in Acres	Acres Per 100 Persons	Area in Acres	Acres Per 100 Persons	Area in Acres	Acres Per 100 Persons
Single-Family Dwellings	1,220.04	7.13	3,589.21	7.62	8,571.85	6.33	9,363.08	1.79	22,744.18	3.14
Two-Family Dwellings	42.05	0.25	107.12	0.23	320.73	0.24	1,610.57	0.31	2,080.47	0.29
Multifamily Dwellings	6.99	0.04	92.03	0.19	278.05	0.20	1,186.89	0.22	1,563.96	0.22
Commercial Areas	140.20	0.82	144.74	0.31	375.08	0.28	937.85	0.18	1,597.87	0.22
Light and Heavy Industry	302.91	1.77	251.27	0.53	286.08	0.21	4,099.12	0.78	4,939.38	0.69
Railroad Property	209.30	1.22	386.85	0.82	543.29	0.40	1,784.98	0.34	2,924.42	0.40
Parks and Playgrounds	138.42	0.81	712.30	1.51	833.47	0.62	1,059.58	0.20	2,743.77	0.38
Public and Semipublic Property	1,056.39	6.17	1,464.65	3.11	2,284.54	1.69	2,065.74	0.40	6,871.32	0.95
Streets	1,504.40	8.79	3,349.34	7.11	4,428.97	3.27	8,113.00	1.55	17,395.71	2.40
Total Developed Area	4,620.70	27.00	10,097.51	21.43	17,922.06	13.24	30,220.81	5.77	62,861.08	8.69
Total Surveyed Area	12,782.07	-	17,646.64	-	28,799.54	-	39,185.19	-	98,413.44	-

TABLE 9. LAND USE IN 11 URBAN AREAS. Percentage of total developed area occupied by major urban uses.

	Urban Areas	Year of Survey	Population[a] At Date of Survey	Single-Family Dwellings		Two-Family Dwellings		Multi-Family Dwellings		Commercial Use		Light Industry	
				Area in Acres	% of Total Developed Area	Area in Acres	% of Total Developed Area	Area in Acres	% of Total Developed Area	Area in Acres	% of Total Developed Area	Area in Acres	% of Total Developed Area
1	Battle Creek, Michigan	1947	67,725	2,430.90	27.99	242.20	2.79	133.80	1.54	403.00	4.64	212.30	2.45
2	Brookhaven, Mississippi	1950	10,820	589.40	37.44	33.60	2.13	23.90	1.52	33.40	2.12	63.00	4.00
3	Corpus Christi, Texas	1951	119,825	4,156.80	33.85	192.60	1.57	252.60	2.06	537.00	4.37	403.30	3.29
4	Frankfort, Kentucky	1951	16,535	501.60	33.84	84.60	5.71	42.40	2.86	39.50	2.66	28.40	1.92
5	Freeport, Illinois	1952	24,637	966.10	38.64	103.30	4.13	32.00	1.28	63.00	2.52	70.40	2.82
6	Jacksonville, Illinois	1949	22,600	1,162.10	38.43	94.80	3.14	67.80	2.24	56.50	1.87	37.70	1.25
7	Jefferson City, Missouri	1952	26,000	1,094.80	23.51	105.50	2.27	47.50	1.02	119.40	2.56	55.90	1.21
8	Lincoln, Nebraska	1951	103,625	3,631.00	19.65	123.00	0.67	142.00	0.77	299.00	1.59	199.00	1.08
9	Sioux Falls, South Dakota	1949	55,000	1,468.40	20.66	106.60	1.50	116.50	1.64	163.60	2.30	159.20	2.24
10	Streator, Illinois	1949	20,720	1,139.20	38.39	42.90	1.45	10.40	0.35	68.80	2.32	35.40	1.19
11	Williamsburg, Virginia	1952	7,150	507.60	6.60	15.90	0.21	57.00	0.74	88.00	1.15	53.20	0.69

[a] Estimated, or interpolated from U. S. Census.

	Urban Areas	Heavy Industry		Railroad Property		Parks And Playgrounds		Public And Semi-Public Property		Streets		Total Development	
		Area in Acres	% of Total Developed Area	Area in Acres	% of Total Developed Area	Area in Acres	% of Total Developed Area	Area in Acres	% of Total Developed Area	Area in Acres	% of Total Developed Area	Area in Acres	
1	Battle Creek, Michigan	291.80	3.36	394.40	4.54	392.90	4.52	2,101.40	24.19	2,083.00	23.98	8,685.70	1
2	Brookhaven, Mississippi	97.90	6.22	128.80	8.18	12.50	0.79	115.20	7.32	476.80	30.28	1,574.50	2
3	Corpus Christi, Texas	1,292.00	10.52	274.70	2.24	414.20	3.37	1,251.20	10.19	3,504.40	28.54	12,278.80	3
4	Frankfort, Kentucky	25.60	1.73	59.10	3.99	3.70	0.25	308.10	20.79	389.10	26.25	1,482.10	4
5	Freeport, Illinois	80.40	3.22	156.80	6.27	223.40	8.93	163.10	6.52	641.70	25.67	2,500.20	5
6	Jacksonville, Illinois	38.50	1.27	135.30	4.47	128.10	4.24	644.80	21.32	658.30	21.77	3,023.90	6
7	Jefferson City, Missouri	39.20	0.84	288.90	6.21	257.50	5.53	721.90	15.50	1,925.50	41.35	4,656.10	7
8	Lincoln, Nebraska	82.00	0.44	2,148.00	11.63	1,237.00	6.69	4,443.00	24.05	6,177.00	33.43	18,475.00	8
9	Sioux Falls, South Dakota	331.00	4.66	397.90	5.60	533.80	7.51	1,934.50	27.22	1,895.50	26.67	7,107.00	9
10	Streator, Illinois	370.80	12.50	251.80	8.49	25.30	0.85	223.50	7.53	799.00	26.93	2,967.10	10
11	Williamsburg, Virginia	8.20	0.11	145.30	1.89	2.90	0.04	5,914.50	76.91	896.90	11.66	7,689.50	11

TABLE 10. LAND USE IN 11 URBAN AREAS. Acres per 100 persons occupied by major urban uses.

	Urban Areas	Year Of Survey	Population[a] At Date Of Survey	Single-Family Dwellings		Two-Family Dwellings		Multi-Family Dwellings		Commercial Use		Light Industry	
				Area In Acres	Acres Per 100 Persons	Area In Acres	Acres Per 100 Persons	Area In Acres	Acres Per 100 Persons	Area In Acres	Acres Per 100 Persons	Area In Acres	Acres Per 100 Persons
1	Battle Creek, Michigan	1947	67,725	2,430.90	3.59	242.20	0.36	133.80	0.20	403.00	0.59	212.30	0.31
2	Brookhaven, Mississippi	1950	10,820	589.40	5.45	33.60	0.31	23.90	0.22	33.40	0.31	63.00	0.58
3	Corpus Christi, Texas	1951	119,825	4,156.80	3.47	192.60	0.16	252.60	0.21	537.00	0.45	403.30	0.34
4	Frankfort, Kentucky	1951	16,535	501.60	3.03	84.60	0.51	42.40	0.26	39.50	0.24	28.40	0.17
5	Freeport, Illinois	1952	24,637	966.10	3.92	103.30	0.42	32.00	0.13	63.00	0.25	70.40	0.29
6	Jacksonville, Illinois	1949	22,600	1,162.10	5.14	94.80	0.42	67.80	0.30	56.50	0.25	37.70	0.17
7	Jefferson City, Missouri	1952	26,000	1,094.80	4.21	105.50	0.41	47.50	0.18	119.40	0.46	55.90	0.21
8	Lincoln, Nebraska	1951	103,625	3,631.00	3.51	123.00	0.12	142.00	0.14	293.00	0.28	199.00	0.19
9	Sioux Falls, South Dakota	1949	55,000	1,468.40	2.67	106.60	0.19	116.50	0.21	163.60	0.30	159.20	0.30
10	Streator, Illinois	1949	20,720	1,139.20	5.50	42.90	0.21	10.40	0.05	68.80	0.33	35.40	0.17
11	Williamsburg, Virginia	1952	7,150	507.60	7.10	15.90	0.22	57.00	0.80	88.00	1.23	53.20	0.75

[a]Estimated, or interpolated from U. S. Census

TABLE 10 (continued). LAND USE IN 11 URBAN AREAS. Acres per 100 persons occupied by major urban uses

	Urban Areas	Heavy Industry		Railroad Property		Parks And Playgrounds		Public And Semi-Public Property		Streets		Total Developed Area		
		Area In Acres	Acres Per 100 Persons	Area In Acres	Acres Per 100 Persons	Area In Acres	Acres Per 100 Persons	Area In Acres	Acres Per 100 Persons	Area In Acres	Acres Per 100 Persons	Area In Acres	Acres Per 100 Persons	
1	Battle Creek, Michigan	291.80	0.43	394.40	0.58	392.90	0.58	2,101.40	3.10	2,083.00	3.08	8,685.70	12.82	1
2	Brookhaven, Mississippi	97.90	0.90	128.80	1.19	12.50	0.12	115.20	1.06	476.80	4.41	1,574.50	14.55	2
3	Corpus Christi, Texas	1,292.00	1.08	274.70	0.23	414.20	0.35	1,251.20	1.04	3,504.40	2.92	12,278.80	10.25	3
4	Frankfort, Kentucky	25.60	0.16	59.10	0.36	3.70	0.02	308.10	1.86	389.10	2.35	1,482.10	8.96	4
5	Freeport, Illinois	80.40	0.33	156.80	0.64	223.40	0.91	163.10	0.66	641.70	2.60	2,500.20	10.15	5
6	Jacksonville, Illinois	38.50	0.17	135.30	0.60	128.10	0.57	644.80	2.85	658.30	2.91	3,023.90	13.38	6
7	Jefferson City, Missouri	39.20	0.15	288.90	1.11	257.50	0.99	721.90	2.78	1,925.50	7.41	4,656.10	17.91	7
8	Lincoln, Nebraska	82.00	0.08	2,148.00	2.07	1,237.00	1.19	4,443.00	4.29	6,177.00	5.96	18,475.00	17.83	8
9	Sioux Falls, South Dakota	331.00	0.60	397.90	0.72	533.80	0.97	1,934.50	3.52	1,895.50	3.44	7,107.00	12.92	9
10	Streator, Illinois	370.80	1.79	251.80	1.21	25.30	0.12	223.50	1.08	799.00	3.86	2,967.10	14.32	10
11	Williamsburg, Virginia	8.20	0.12	145.30	2.03	2.90	0.04	5,914.50	82.72	896.90	12.54	7,689.50	107.55	11

TABLE 11. LAND USE IN 11 URBAN AREAS. Percentage of total developed area and acres per 100 persons occupied by major urban uses.

Type of Use	All Population Groups 11 Urban Areas		
	Area in Acres	Percent of Total Developed Area	Acres Per 100 Persons
Single-Family Dwellings	17,647.90	25.05	3.72
Two-Family Dwellings	1,145.00	1.63	0.24
Multifamily Dwellings	925.90	1.31	0.20
Commercial Areas	1,865.20	2.65	0.39
Light Industry	1,317.80	1.87	0.28
Heavy Industry	2,657.40	3.77	0.56
Railroad Property	4,381.00	6.22	0.92
Parks and Playgrounds	3,231.30	4.59	0.68
Public and Semipublic Property	17,821.20	25.30	3.75
Streets	19,447.20	27.61	4.10
Total Developed Area	70,439.90	100.00	14.84

TABLE 12.   COMPARISON OF EXISTING AND PROPOSED ZONING DISTRICTS.   Hutchinson, Kansas.

Use District	AREA USED		AREA NOW ZONED		PROPOSED ZONES	
	Acres	Percent	Acres	Percent	Acres	Percent
Single-Family Dwellings	1299.1	30.5			2118.8	49.8
Two-Family Dwellings	66.1	1.6			469.8	11.0
Multi-Family Dwellings	65.8	1.5			351.5	8.3
Total Dwelling Area	1431.0	33.6	2197.4	51.6	2940.1	69.1
Commercial	76.0	1.8	330.4	7.7	160.7	3.7
Light Industry	78.0	1.8	555.5		479.8	11.2
Heavy Industry	145.2	3.4	1180.4		683.2	16.0
Railroads	143.9	3.4				
Total Industry	367.1	8.6	1735.9	40.7	1163.0	27.2
Public and Semipublic	616.4	14.5				
Parks and Playgrounds	322.7	7.5				
Vacant	1450.6	34.0				
Total Area Zoned	4263.8	100.0	4263.7	100.0	4263.8	100.0

TABLE 13. COMPARATIVE DATA, 1932 and 1953. Computed on the 1932 basis.

Use	Central Cities				Satellite Cities			
	Percent of Total Developed Area		Acres Per 100 Persons		Percent of Total Developed Area		Acres Per 100 Persons	
	Sixteen Cities (1932 Study)	Fifty-Three Cities (1953 Study)	Sixteen Cities (1932 Study)	Fifty-Three Cities (1953 Study)	Six Cities (1932 Study)	Thirty-Three Cities (1953 Study)	Six Cities (1932 Study)	Thirty-Three Cities (1953 Study)
Single-Family Dwellings	36.10	33.54	2.94	3.42	44.50	39.31	4.68	5.91
Two-Family Dwellings	2.10	4.15	0.14	0.35	1.95	2.91	0.18	0.27
Multifamily Dwellings	1.09	2.19	0.08	0.21	1.71	2.42	0.12	0.18
Commercial Areas	2.38	3.25	0.18	0.35	1.43	2.50	0.13	0.37
Light Industry	11.41	11.02	0.92	1.04	10.79	9.74	1.17	1.44
Heavy Industry								
Railroad Property								
Parks and Playgrounds	6.33	5.41	0.48	0.47	1.26	3.84	0.11	0.92
Public and Semipublic Property	7.61	12.48	0.62	1.59	9.13	11.36	1.01	2.40
Streets	33.60	28.24	2.82	3.03	29.70	27.92	3.01	4.77
Total	100.62	100.28	8.18	10.45	100.47	100.00	10.41	16.26

All calculations are "mean averages"; see note on method. These data are not indicative of trends.

TABLE 14. COMPARATIVE DATA, 1932 and 1953. Computed on the 1953 basis.

Use	Central Cities				Satellite Cities			
	Percent of Total Developed Area		Acres Per 100 Persons		Percent of Total Developed Area		Acres Per 100 Persons	
	Sixteen Cities (1932 Study)	Fifty-Three Cities (1953 Study)	Sixteen Cities (1932 Study)	Fifty-Three Cities (1953 Study)	Six Cities (1932 Study)	Thirty-Three Cities (1953 Study)	Six Cities (1932 Study)	Thirty-Three Cities (1953 Study)
Single-Family Dwellings	36.78	31.81	2.61	2.19	44.12	36.18	3.61	3.14
Two-Family Dwellings	1.87	4.79	0.13	0.33	2.03	3.31	0.17	0.29
Multifamily Dwellings	1.23	3.01	0.09	0.21	2.28	2.49	0.19	0.22
Commercial Areas	2.41	3.32	0.17	0.23	1.57	2.54	0.13	0.22
Light Industry	⎱10.38	11.30	0.74	0.78	6.78	12.51	0.55	1.09
Heavy Industry	⎰							
Railroad Property								
Parks and Playgrounds	7.09	6.74	0.50	0.46	1.69	4.37	0.14	0.38
Public and Semipublic Property	7.59	10.93	0.54	0.75	10.33	10.93	0.84	0.95
Streets	32.65	28.10	2.31	1.94	31.19	27.67	2.55	2.40
Total	100.00	100.00	7.09	6.89	100.00	100.00	8.18	8.69

All calculations are simple arithmetic averages; see note on method. These data are not indicative of trends.